Frommer's®

New Orleans
day BY day™

1st Edition

by Julia Kamysz Lane

Wiley Publishing, Inc.

Contents

Published by:
Wiley Publishing, Inc.

111 River St.
Hoboken, NJ 07030-5774

ISBN 978-0-470-48726-6

Editor: Cate Latting, with special thanks to Mary Herczog
Production Editor: Eric T. Schroeder
Photo Editor: Richard Fox
Cartographer: Guy Ruggiero
Production by Wiley Indianapolis Composition Services

For information on our other products and services or to obtain technical support, please contact our Customer Care Department within the U.S. at 877/762-2974, outside the U.S. at 317/572-3993 or fax 317/572-4002. Wiley also publishes its books in a variety of electronic formats. Some content that appears in print may not be available in electronic formats.

Manufactured in China

5 4 3 2

A Note from the Editorial Director

Organizing your time. That's what this guide is all about.

Other guides give you long lists of things to see and do and then expect you to fit the pieces together. The Day by Day guides are different. These guides tell you the best of everything, and then they show you how to see it *in the smartest, most time-efficient way.* Our authors have designed detailed itineraries organized by time, neighborhood, or special interest. And each tour comes with a bulleted map that takes you from stop to stop.

Hoping to soak in the history of the French Quarter, visit some underwater friends at the Aquarium of the Americas, or see where some of the U.S.'s most famous writers spent their time and spun their tales? Planning a walk through the Garden District, or dinner and drinks where you can dance the night away to a local jazz or brass band? Whatever your interest or schedule, the Day by Days give you the smartest routes to follow. Not only do we take you to the top attractions, hotels, and restaurants, but we also help you access those special moments that locals get to experience—those "finds" that turn tourists into travelers.

The Day by Days are also your top choice if you're looking for one complete guide for all your travel needs. The best hotels and restaurants for every budget, the greatest shopping values, the wildest nightlife—it's all here.

Why should you trust our judgment? Because our authors personally visit each place they write about. They're an independent lot who say what they think and would never include places they wouldn't recommend to their best friends. They're also open to suggestions from readers. If you'd like to contact them, please send your comments our way at feedback@frommers.com, and we'll pass them on.

Enjoy your Day by Day guide—the most helpful travel companion you can buy. And have the trip of a lifetime.

Warm regards,

Kelly Regan

Kelly Regan, Editorial Director
Frommer's Travel Guides

About the Author

Julia Kamysz Lane divides her time between a 1940's cottage in New Orleans and an old farmhouse in northern Illinois. She and her husband share a love of Southern cooking, historic architecture, books, and the endless entertainment provided by five dogs and two cats.

An Additional Note

Please be advised that travel information is subject to change at any time—and this is especially true of prices. We therefore suggest that you write or call ahead for confirmation when making your travel plans. The authors, editors, and publisher cannot be held responsible for the experiences of readers while traveling. Your safety is important to us, however, so we encourage you to stay alert and be aware of your surroundings.

Star Ratings, Icons & Abbreviations

Every hotel, restaurant, and attraction listing in this guide has been ranked for quality, value, service, amenities, and special features using a **star-rating system.** Hotels, restaurants, attractions, shopping, and nightlife are rated on a scale of zero stars (recommended) to three stars (exceptional). In addition to the star-rating system, we also use a **kids icon** to point out the best bets for families. Within each tour, we recommend cafes, bars, or restaurants where you can take a break. Each of these stops appears in a shaded box marked with a coffee-cup-shaped bullet ☕.

The following **abbreviations** are used for credit cards:

AE	American Express	**DISC**	Discover	**V**	Visa
DC	Diners Club	**MC**	MasterCard		

Travel Resources at Frommers.com

Frommer's travel resources don't end with this guide. Frommer's website, **www.frommers.com,** has travel information on more than 4,000 destinations. We update features regularly, giving you access to the most current trip-planning information and the best airfare, lodging, and car-rental bargains. You can also listen to podcasts, connect with other Frommers.com members through our active-reader forums, share your travel photos, read blogs from guidebook editors and fellow travelers, and much more.

A Note on Prices

In the "Take a Break" and "Best Bets" sections of this book, we have used a system of dollar signs to show a range of costs for 1 night in a hotel (the price of a double-occupancy room) or the cost of an entree at a restaurant. Use the following table to decipher the dollar signs:

Cost	Hotels	Restaurants
$	under $100	under $10
$$	$100–$200	$10–$20
$$$	$200–$300	$20–$30
$$$$	$300–$400	$30–$40
$$$$$	over $400	over $40

How to Contact Us

In researching this book, we discovered many wonderful places—hotels, restaurants, shops, and more. We're sure you'll find others. Please tell us about them, so we can share the information with your fellow travelers in upcoming editions. If you were disappointed with a recommendation, we'd love to know that, too. Please write to:

Frommer's New Orleans, Day by Day, 1st Edition
Wiley Publishing, Inc. • 111 River St. • Hoboken, NJ 07030-5774

16 Favorite
Moments

16 Favorite **Moments**

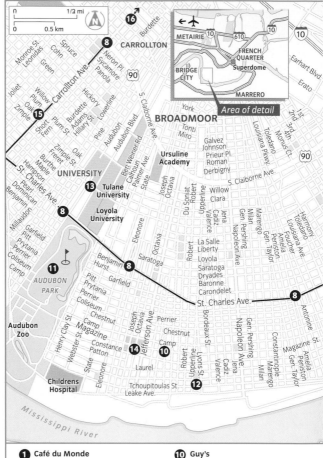

1 Café du Monde
2 Jackson Square
3 Le Petit Theatre
4 Ferry to Algiers Point
5 Snug Harbor
6 Napoleon House
7 National World War II Museum
8 St. Charles Streetcar
9 Mardi Gras Parade
  (not mapped; see p.34)

10 Guy's
11 Audubon Park
12 Hansen's Sno Bliz
13 The Mushroom
14 Magazine Street shops
15 rue de la course
16 Mid City Rock 'n' Bowl

Previous page: Jackson Square with the Cabildo, St. Louis Cathedral, and the Presbytere (from left to right) in the background.

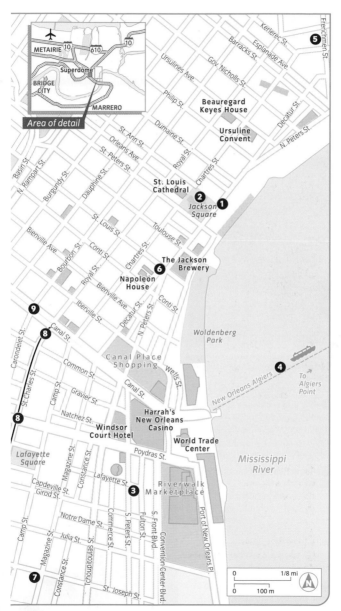

METAIRIE

Superdome

BRIDGE CITY

MARRERO

Area of detail

Kerlerec St.

Esplanade Ave

Barracks St.

Frenchmen St.

5

Ursulines Ave.

Gov. Nicholls St.

Decatur St.

Philip St.

Beauregard
Keyes House

N. Peters St.

Dumaine St.

Ursuline
Convent

St. Ann St.

Orleans Ave.

St. Peters St.

Royal St.

Chartres St.

Basin St.

N. Rampart St.

Burgundy St.

Dauphine St.

St. Louis
Cathedral

2

1
Jackson
Square

St. Louis St.

Toulouse St.

Bienville Ave.

Bourbon St.

Conti St.

Chartres St.

The Jackson
Brewery

6

Royal St.

Napoleon
House

Bienville Ave.

Conti St.

Woldenberg
Park

Iberville St.

Decatur St.

N. Peters St.

9

Canal St.

8

Canal St.

Carondelet St.

Common St.

Canal Place
Shopping

Wells St.

New Orleans Algiers

4
To
Algiers
Point

St. Charles St.

Camp St.

Gravier St.

Canal St.

8

Natchez St.

Harrah's
New Orleans
Casino

Windsor
Court Hotel

World Trade
Center

Mississippi
River

Lafayette
Square

Magazine St.

Constance St.

Poydras St.

Lafayette St.

Capdeville St.

Girod St.

3

Riverwalk
Marketplace

Notre Dame St.

Commerce St.

S. Peters St.

Fulton St.

S. Front Blvd.

Convention Center Blvd.

Port of New Orleans Pl.

Camp St.

Magazine St.

Julia St.

Tchoupitoulas St.

Constance St.

7

St. Joseph St.

0   1/8 mi

0   100 m

Why is New Orleans called the "City That Care Forgot"? Because it's easy to forget your troubles while swaying with the crowd at a parade or feasting on fresh seafood in a little family joint. All of your senses are exhilarated by the spirit of the Crescent City, from the soulful notes of a saxophone to gentle drops of rain cooling you off on a warm afternoon. Locals are famous for welcoming visitors as one of their own and inviting them to indulge in everything New Orleans has to offer. So don't be afraid to let loose and *laissez les bon temps rouler!* For ideas on how to start doing just that, check out some of my favorite New Orleans moments below.

Passengers aboard the ferry to Algiers Point enjoy views of the New Orleans skyline.

❶ **Bite into a beignet at world-famous Café du Monde.** Getting coated in powdered sugar never tasted so good! Don't forget the creamy café au lait. *See p 48.*

❷ **People-watch in Jackson Square.** Stroll the heart of the French Quarter, which pulses night and day with talented street musicians, eclectic artists, funny mimes, and passionate fortune tellers. Most of the entertainment is free, but if you like what you see or hear, drop a few coins in the hat. *See p 9.*

❸ **Enjoy a performance at Le Petit Theatre,** housed in an intimate, 1920s Spanish-styled dwelling with cushy red seats to sink into. The nearly 100-year-old community theater is renowned for classics by southern playwrights such as Tennessee Williams. *See p 131.*

❹ **Ferry across the Mississippi River to Algiers Point,** one of New Orleans' oldest suburbs and home to jazz pioneers, for a dramatic perspective on the city skyline. *See p 93.*

❺ **Snap your fingers to live jazz at Snug Harbor,** the place to hear legends like pianist Ellis Marsalis, father of Pulitzer Prize–winning trumpeter Wynton Marsalis, and power vocalist Charmaine Neville. *See p 120.*

❻ **Say cheers with a Pimm's Cup at Napoleon House,** a 200-year-old manor once offered by New Orleans mayor Nicholas Girod as refuge for

A bust of Napoleon sits above the cash register at Napoleon House.

A ride on the St. Charles streetcar is a fun and cheap way to get a passing veiw of the Garden District.

the exiled French emperor. Napoleon never took up Mayor Girod on his hospitality, but a bust in his likeness serves as fine company for the artists and writers who aspire to take over the world. *See p 120.*

7 Climb into a Higgins landing craft at the National World War II Museum. The boat that made victory possible on D-Day was invented and built in New Orleans and tested on the brackish waters of Lake Pontchartrain. *See p 81.*

8 Ride the St. Charles Streetcar. Marvel at the world-famous Avenue's historic mansions, universities, churches, and temples. There's no better way to cool off on a warm day than the breeze through a streetcar window as you travel beneath a canopy of sweeping live oaks. *See p 17.*

9 Yell "throw me something, mister!" at a Mardi Gras parade. Then test your hand-eye coordination while catching beads, doubloons, and other throws. Remember that beads begat beads, so throw a few pearls around your neck before you hear the police car sirens announcing the start of the parade. *See p 35.*

10 Savor the signature grilled shrimp po' boy at Guy's, a small family-run place favored by locals.

Grab a bottle of Barq's from the corner cooler and glance through *Gambit*, the local alternative newspaper, while you wait for your freshly made order. *See p 105.*

11 Stroll through Audubon Park and look for wood ducks, egrets, cranes, and sunbathing turtles that plop back into the water if you get too close. The still lagoons and sprawling live oaks dripping with Spanish moss make for a particularly romantic scene. *See p 60.*

A member of the Zulus prepares to make his "throws."

No one can resist a snoball from Hansen's Sno Bliz.

⓬ Cool off with a snoball at Hansen's Sno Bliz. No slushies or slurpies here! The late Mary's original syrups make for endlessly sticky sweet (or sour) combinations. *See p 105.*

⓭ Flip through vintage vinyl at The Mushroom, a beloved 39-year-old independent record store on the edge of Tulane University's campus. One look at the psychedelic entrance mural and thousands of new and used CDs, LPs, and DVDs, and you'll agree with the store's motto that "It's worth the trip!" *See p 82.*

⓮ Explore the shops of Magazine Street, 6 glorious miles (9.6km) of antiques, books, vintage clothing, and more. I have yet to meet any shopaholic who can go the distance in one day, but you'll have fun trying. *See p 18.*

⓯ Sip an Iced Cioccolato at rue de la course, one of my favorite independent coffeehouses ever. It's located in a cavernous former bank at Carrollton and Oak that features a second-story loft from which you can better view the 19th-century architectural details and unusually eclectic patrons. *See p 72.*

⓰ Bowl to live Zydeco music at Mid City Rock 'n' Bowl. It's not much to look at from the outside, but go up the steps to discover a unique venue where you can dance, drink, and bowl all at the same time. *See p 15.* ●

Rue de la Course is a delightful coffee shop housed in a former bank building.

1

The Best
Full-Day Tours

The Best **in One Day**

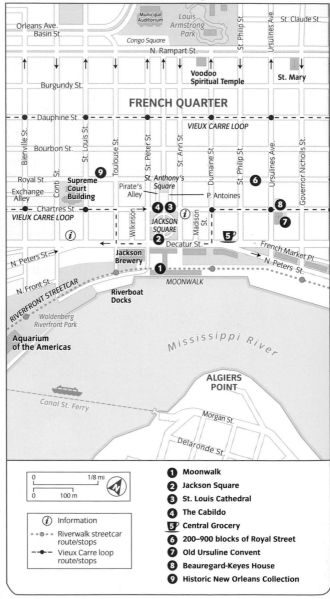

1. Moonwalk
2. Jackson Square
3. St. Louis Cathedral
4. The Cabildo
5. Central Grocery
6. 200–900 blocks of Royal Street
7. Old Ursuline Convent
8. Beauregard-Keyes House
9. Historic New Orleans Collection

Previous page: A trumpet player blows his horn in front of St. Louis Cathedral.

If you only have 1 day in New Orleans, go to the heart of the city, the world-famous French Quarter. As you walk under wrought-iron balconies and steal glances through brick arches to private court-yards, you'll let go of everyday concerns and embrace a simpler time. Here, you can find anything you desire, from fine cuisine to elegant antiques. START: **Moonwalk, across from Jackson Square.**

① kids Moonwalk. The sleepy riverside park, which winds along the Mississippi River, is a tribute to former Mayor Moon Landrieu, during whose administration it was built. ⏲ *20 min. Across from Jackson Square along Mississippi River.* ☎ *504/587-0738. Go before 8pm for safety's sake.*

② ★ kids Jackson Square. In the days when it was known as the Place d'Armes, military parades and public executions were common. On November 30, 1803, citizens gathered here to learn that Louisi-ana was once again a French pos-session. But less than a month later, the crowd was told of the famous Louisiana Purchase, marking Ameri-ca's cheapest and largest land grab of all time. These days, you'll find artists displaying paintings and drawings, palm readers telling fortunes, and little kids tap-dancing for spare change. ⏲ *30 min.–1 hr. Fronts the 700 block of Decatur St. and is bounded by Chartres, St. Ann, and St. Peter sts. www.jackson-square.com. Dawn–dusk.*

A sign in Jackson Square noting the former Spanish name of the square, Plaza de Armas.

③ ★★ St. Louis Cathedral. New Orleans is home to one of the South's largest Catholic populations and boasts the oldest continuously operating cathedral in the United States. This is the third building to have stood on this spot; a 1722 hur-ricane demolished the first and the great fire of 1788 burned the sec-ond. Supposedly, the church's bells were not rung as a warning of the fire because it was Good Friday. ⏲ *20 min. 615 Pere Antoine Alley.*

A display case exhibiting relics of old New Orleans in the Cabildo.

Shop signs along Royal street.

☎ 504/525-9585. www.stlouis cathedral.org. Mon–Sat 8am–4pm, closed Sun. Mass schedule online.

④ ★ The Cabildo. Originally built in 1795 as the Spanish seat of government, this is the site where the French government turned over the Louisiana Purchase to the United States in 1803. Despite the ravages of time and a fire in the 1980s, the Cabildo lives on, educating visitors on what it took to survive in 18th-century

Preparing the famous muffuletta sandwiches at Central Grocery.

Louisiana. 🕐 1 hr. 701 Chartres St. ☎ 800/568-6968 or 504/568-6968. http://lsm.crt.state.la.us/cabex.htm. Amission $6 adults, $5 students and seniors, free children 12 and under. Tues–Sun 9am–5pm.

⑤ Central Grocery. Stop by this grocery for one of its famously filling muffuletta sandwiches. You can also buy many New Orleans spices and other deli items here as well. 923 Decatur St. ☎ 504/523-1620. $.

⑥ 200–900 blocks of Royal Street. If rowdy Bourbon Street is the black sheep of the French Quarter, then Royal Street is its prim and proper cousin boasting fine art galleries, antiques shops, women's clothing boutiques, and home accessory nooks. For a detailed map of shops along Royal Street, turn to p. 75. 🕐 90 min.

⑦ ★★ Old Ursuline Convent. Built between 1745 and 1752, the convent was once run by the Sisters of Ursula, who came to New Orleans from France in 1727 and were the first to open a girls-only school in the United States. From 1831 to 1834, the Louisiana state legislature was based here. Today,

it houses a Catholic archive with documents dating back to 1718.
🕑 1–1½ hr. 1100 Chartres St. ☎ 504/529-3040. Admission $5 adults, $4 seniors, $2 students. Tues–Fri 10am–3pm, Sat–Sun 11am–3pm. Tours Tues–Fri 10am, 11am, 1pm, 2pm, and 3pm; Sat–Sun 11:15am, 1pm, and 2pm.

⑧ ★ Beauregard-Keyes House. Built in 1826, this stunning, raised Greek Revival home is named for its most famous tenants: Confederate General Pierre Gustave Toutant Beauregard, who resided here after the Civil War, and author Frances Parkinson Keyes (pronounced Cause), who wrote many of her novels here, including the most famous, *Dinner at Antoine's*. The landscaped courtyard opens to the former servants' quarters, where Keyes maintained her writing space. The beautifully restored formal garden is a breathtaking oasis. Note the twin staircases, Doric columns, and the "raised cottage" architecture.
🕑 1 hr. 1113 Chartres St. ☎ 504/523-7257. Admission $5 adults, $4 students and seniors, $2 children

Historic New Orleans Collection.

6–12, free children 5 and under. Mon–Sat 10am–3pm.

⑨ ★ Historic New Orleans Collection. A complex of late-18th-century and early-19th-century buildings tells the story of New Orleans' past and present through changing exhibits on art, food, architecture, music, and more.
🕑 45 min. 533 Royal St. ☎ 504/523-4662. www.hnoc.org. Free admission for self-guided tours. Small fee for docent tours. Call ahead for price. Tues–Sat 10am–4:30pm.

Inside the Beauregard-Keyes House.

The Best **in Two Days**

1. City Park
2. New Orleans Museum of Art
3. New Orleans Botanical Garden
4. Bayou St. John
5. Pitot House
6. Bayou Coffee House & Wine Bar
7. Canal Streetcar
8. Cypress Grove & Greenwood cemeteries
9. Lake Lawn Cemetery
10. Mid City Rock 'n' Bowl

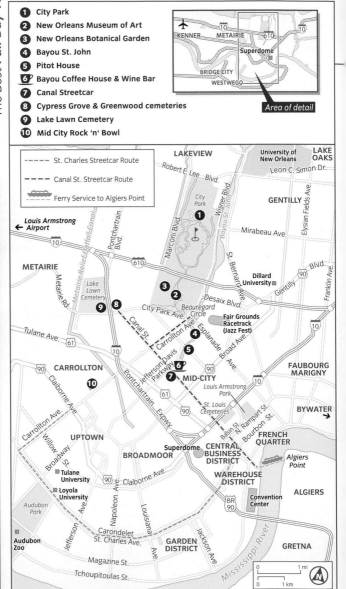

Area of detail

----- St. Charles Streetcar Route

- - - Canal St. Streetcar Route

Ferry Service to Algiers Point

From the feel-good food to the thought-provoking art and architecture, Mid-City is where it's at, y'all. The Mid-City neighborhood was devastated by Hurricane Katrina flooding in 2005, but walking among homes, schools, and businesses in various stages of renewal, you'll get a feel for what New Orleans is all about—community spirit, tenacity, and pride. START: **Canal Streetcar, City Park/Museum car.**

❶ ★★ **City Park.** Play golf or tennis, or go horseback riding, fishing, birding, or boating. Kids will clamor to go on the antique wooden carousel at the Carousel Gardens Amusement Park or climb through, over, and under the fairy-tale sculptures at Storyland. See p 88. ◷ *1 hr. 1 Palm Dr.; bounded by City Park Ave. and Canal, Lee, and Wisner boulevards. ☎ 504/482-4888. www.neworleans citypark.com. Open daily.*

❷ **New Orleans Museum of Art.** City Park's main oak-lined entrance also leads directly to NOMA, home to priceless paintings, ceramics, and sculptures, and one of the largest fine photography collections in the region. ◷ *2–3 hr. 1 Collins Diboll Circle. ☎ 504/658-4100. www.noma.org. Admission $8 adults, $7 seniors and students with I.D., $4 children 3–17, free children 2 and under. Tues–Sun 10am–4:30pm.*

City Park.

New Orleans Botanical Garden.

❸ **kids New Orleans Botanical Garden.** Originally created as part of the Works Progress Administration in the 1930s, this public garden is one of the few in existence from the Great Depression/Art Deco period. Explore 12 acres (4.8 hectares) of gardens, fountains, ponds, and sculptures, plus a horticultural library and a gift shop. Kids of all ages will especially enjoy the miniature train garden (only on weekends). ◷ *1 hr. Pavilion of the Two Sisters on Victory Ave., behind the New Orleans Museum of Art. ☎ 504/483-9386. Admission $6 adults, $3 children 5–12, free for children 4 and under. Tues–Sat 10am–4:30pm.*

As you leave City Park, cross Wisner Boulevard and go over the bridge. Turn right on Moss Street and you'll be on the west side of Bayou St. John.

❹ ★ **Bayou St. John.** This historic waterway once connected Lake Pontchartrain to the Mississippi

Bayou St. John.

River, serving as an important channel for Native Americans and later, European explorers. Modern development swallowed up parts of the bayou, so it no longer connects the two. What remains serves as a popular recreational spot for fishing, canoeing, and bird-watching. See p 66. 🕐 *30 min.*

⑤ ★ Pitot House. Enter the romantic grounds of this 18th-century Creole colonial house museum and you can easily imagine the lives of New Orleans' earliest settlers. The city's first American mayor, James Pitot, lived here from 1810 to 1819. Back then, it was considered to be a country home, which gives you an idea of how much development the bayou spawned over the past two centuries. 🕐 *1 hr. 1440*

Moss St. ☎ 504/482-0312. Admission $7 adults, $5 students, senior, and children 7–18, free children 6 and under. Wed–Sat 10am–3pm.

⑥ Bayou Coffee House & Wine Bar. At the end of the bayou, you'll find a bright pink house and cozy outdoor seating where you can sip an iced coffee or something stronger (hey, you're not driving!). Breakfast is served all day, so go ahead and order those oh-so-good, oh-so-greasy bacon grits. Note: Closed on Thursdays. *326 N Jefferson Davis Pkwy.* ☎ *504/484-7390. $.*

⑦ ★ kids Canal Streetcar. Unlike the historic St. Charles line, the Canal cars are bright red and feature air-conditioning and wheelchair access. They might lack character, but that cool air will feel good on a hot, humid afternoon. Be sure to grab the car that says "Cemeteries." 🕐 *30 min.* ☎ *504/248-3900.*

⑧ ★ Cypress Grove & Greenwood cemeteries. Firemen's Charitable & Benevolent Association founded Cypress Grove Cemetery in 1840 to honor its courageous volunteer firemen. At the entrance, you'll

Family tombs at Cypress Grove Cemetery.

A band plays at Mid City Rock 'n' Bowl, a beloved New Orleans institution.

find the massive 1840 vaults of Perseverance Fire Co. No. 13. The yellow fever epidemic of 1852 hit New Orleans particularly hard; Greenwood Cemetery was opened that same year to alleviate crowding at Cypress Grove. Both cemeteries contain some of the finest memorial architecture in the world, featuring marble, granite, and cast-iron tombs. ⏱ *90 min. 5200 Canal Blvd.* ☎ *504/482-8983. www.greenwood nola.com. Free admission. Daily 8am–4pm.*

➒ ★★ Lake Lawn Cemetery. If you enter the city via I-10, you'll have a perfect view of one of the wealthiest, albeit youngest, area cemeteries. On foot, walk among elaborate individual grave sites and enormous marble family tombs encircled by cast-iron fencing and watched over by weeping stone angels. See p 23, ➏.

⏱ *90 min. 5100 Pontchartrain Blvd.* ☎ *504/486-6331. www.lakelawn metairie.com.*

Sometimes, cabs are available on Canal Boulevard beside Cypress Grove and Greenwood cemeteries. Rather than take a chance, call a cab company such as United Cabs (☎ 504/522-9771) to arrange for a pick-up time beforehand at Lake Lawn Cemetery or call them from your cellphone if you're not sure how long you'll want to explore the cities of the dead.

➓ ★★★ Mid City Rock 'n' Bowl. You're guaranteed to pass a good time bowling (and drinking) to live music among locals of all ages and the occasional celebrity like Mick Jagger and Tom Cruise. ⏱ *90 min. 3000 S. Carrollton Ave.* ☎ *504/861-1700. www.rockand bowl.com. Tues–Sat 5–11pm.*

The Best **in Three Days**

1 St. Charles Streetcar
2 Garden District
3 Still Perkin'
4 Lafayette Cemetery No. 1
5 Magazine Street
6 Audubon Zoo
7 Audubon Park

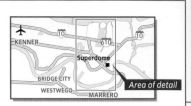

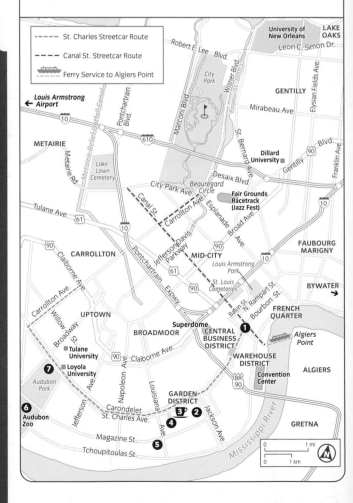

- - - - - St. Charles Streetcar Route

- - - - Canal St. Streetcar Route

Ferry Service to Algiers Point

On your third day in New Orleans, I insist you get out of the Quarter. Many visitors miss out on the fabulous food, historic homes, and southern hospitality found in other close-knit neighborhoods. The Garden District and Uptown both boast manicured mansions, sprawling live oak trees, colorful gardens year-round, eclectic restaurants, and boutique shopping along Magazine Street. After a day of exploring the city's greener side, you can return to the Quarter for more live music and revelry. START: **St. Charles Streetcar at Canal and Carondelet streets.**

① ★★★ kids **St. Charles Streetcar.** From 1835 to 1893, the St. Charles Streetcar line was mule-driven. It went electric in the late 19th century. The present streetcars date from the 1920s and are listed on the National Register of Historic Places. If you have more than three people in your party and the streetcar isn't full, you can pull the back of one wooden bench so two benches face one another for a cozy tête-à-tête. ⏱ *30 min.–2 hr. Canal and Carondelet sts. or any stop along the route following St. Charles and Carrollton aves.*

② ★★ **Garden District.** You can opt for a guided walking tour or DIY; either way, you'll be transfixed by the exclusive estates and lush gardens originally created by rich Americans who weren't welcome by Creole society. See the full Garden District neighborhood walk, p 54. ⏱ *90 min. Bounded by Magazine St. and St. Charles, Jackson, and Louisiana aves.*

③ **Still Perkin'.** Located among the Rink shops, this casual corner coffee spot is known for fresh bagels and unique spreads. *2727 Prytania St.* ☎ *504/899-0335. $.*

④ ★ **Lafayette Cemetery No. 1.** Despite its location in the Garden District, please do not venture into Lafayette on your own; only go with a tour group. This small historic cemetery is best known as the fictional resting place for Anne Rice's beloved vampire Lestat and it was featured in the film *Interview with*

A ride on the St. Charles streetcar should be on every visitor's to-do list.

Streetcar Dollars & Sense

Before you hop on the streetcar, note: A one-way fare is $1.25 (exact change required); a **VisiTour** pass provides unlimited rides on streetcars or buses at a cost of $5 for 1 day or $12 for 3 days. Ask at your hotel or a tourist office for the nearest VisiTour pass vendor, or contact the **New Orleans Regional Transit Authority** (☎ 504/248-3900; www.norta.com).

the Vampire. ⏱ *30 min. 1400 block of Washington Ave.* ☎ *504/525-3377. www.saveourcemeteries.org. Suggested donation $6 adults. Daylight hours only. Closed some holidays.*

5 ★★ **Magazine Street.** Shopaholics could easily spend all day wandering along 6 miles (9.7km) of boutique stores, antiques shops, art galleries, and restaurants. ⏱ *2–3 hr. Bookended by Canal St. and Audubon Park.*

6 **kids** **Audubon Zoo.** Though maybe not as flashy as younger zoos, the exhibits offer a glimpse at many subtropical species that flourish in

the city's heat and humidity. Kids will get a kick out of the underwater view of the silly sea lions. ⏱ *3 hr. 6500 Magazine St. See p. 86,* **3**.

7 ★★★ **kids** **Audubon Park.** Watch wildlife from a bench along the lagoons or turn the kids loose on the playground. Other recreational activities including jogging, golf, tennis, and horseback riding. For more on Audubon Park, see p. 84. ⏱ *45 min. 6500 St. Charles Ave. (across from Tulane and Loyola universities, nestled btw. St. Charles Ave. & Magazine St.).* ☎ *504/581-4629. Daily 6am–10pm.* ●

The shops along Magazine Street.

Cemeteries: Cities of the Dead

1 Our Lady of Guadalupe Chapel and International Shrine of St. Jude
2 St. Louis Cemetery No. 1
3 St. Louis Cemetery No. 3
4 Terranova's
5 Cypress Grove & Greenwood cemeteries
6 Lake Lawn Cemetery
7 Lafayette Cemetery No. 1

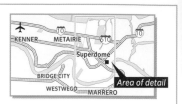

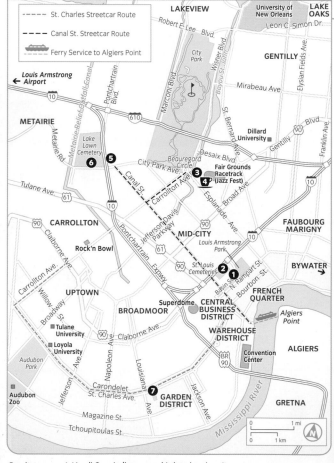

----- St. Charles Streetcar Route
---- Canal St. Streetcar Route
Ferry Service to Algiers Point

Previous page: A Mardi Gras Indian wears his handmade suit.

Ｎew Orleans' famous "Cities of the Dead" are both impressive and practical—it's impossible to have traditional underground graves when much of the city is below sea level. The similarity to the famed Père-Lachaise cemetery in Paris, though, lends credence to some historians' insistence that the aboveground tombs were merely built in the French and Spanish tradition. In the 1990s, thieves regularly stole cemetery statues of angels and saints and other decorative pieces such as urns and wrought-iron fences to sell to antiques dealers around the world for big money. Local citizens and police have made a concerted effort to stop cemetery criminals, but it's a difficult task securing hundreds of thousands of graves and tombs throughout the city. Please be respectful of these sacred spaces. START: **Our Lady of Guadalupe Chapel, 411 N. Rampart St.**

---

❶ Our Lady of Guadalupe Chapel and International Shrine of St. Jude. The small chapel was built in 1826, preceding the more famous and grand St. Louis Cathedral by a good 25 years. Its initial purpose was to serve as a funeral church for the many victims of three yellow fever epidemics in the early 19th century. Today, many visitors travel a great distance in to pray to St. Jude, patron for hopeless and impossible cases, as a last resort to heal terminal illness. ⏱ *20 min. 411 N. Rampart St.* ☎ *504/525-1551. www.saintjude shrine.com. Donations welcome. Daily 7am–7pm.*

❷ ★★ St. Louis Cemetery No. 1. For your safety, please do not enter the city's oldest and most famous cemetery unless you're with a guided tour group. Opened in 1789 after most of the French Quarter burned the year before, some famous locals buried here include the city's first mayor Etienne de Boré, civil rights pioneer Homer Plessy, first African-American mayor Ernest "Dutch" Morial, and world-champion chess player Paul Morphy. The most popular landmark is the Glapion family crypt, where revered (and feared) voodoo priestess Marie Laveau was supposedly

laid to rest. To this day, followers mark her tomb with three small Xs, hoping she will grant them a wish. Needless to say, desecrating any tomb is rude. For more information on Marie Laveau, see the box "The Voodoo Queen of Bayou St. John" on p. 68. ⏱ *1 hr. Basin Street Station Visitors Center, 501 Basin St.* ☎ *504/525-3377. www.saveour cemeteries.org. Suggested donation $12 adults, $10 seniors, $6 students, free children 11 and under. Mon–Sat 9am–3pm, Sun 9am–noon. Tours Sun 10am. Closed holidays.*

The supposed tomb of Marie Laveau at St. Louis Cemetery No. 1.

A simple sign marking Cypress Grove Cemetery.

Take the Canal Streetcar to City Park, then cross Bayou St. John to continue east on Esplanade Avenue.

3 ★ **St. Louis Cemetery No. 3.** Imposing cast-iron gates welcome you inside, where you'll find dramatic angel sculptures and elaborate aboveground tombs for some of the city's most distinguished Creole families. Established in 1854, the cemetery first opened 1 year after the city's worst yellow fever epidemic and began to fill quickly. Keep an eye out for tombs of prominent local figures such as legendary Storyville photographer Ernest Bellocq, missionary priest Father Adrian Rouquette, and free person of color and philanthropist Thomy Lafon, who willed $600,000 to various charities upon his death. One of the most moving tributes can be found on the Gallier family tomb. Architect James Gallier, Jr., designed the cenotaph in memory of his Irish-born architect father, James Gallier, Sr., and his stepmother, Catherine Maria Robinson, who perished together when their steamship sank on its journey from New York to New Orleans on October 3, 1866. The cemetery is clean and well maintained because it continues to be active. In fact, there is a waiting list to buy burial space. ⏱ *30 min. 3421 Esplanade Ave.* ☎ *504/596-3050 or 504/482-5065. www.saveourcemeteries.org. Free admission. Mon–Sat 9am–3pm, Sun 9am–noon. Closed holidays.*

Walk back to City Park and take the Canal Streetcar to the cemeteries at the end of Canal.

4 **Terranova's.** Take a break from the dead and revive yourself with an ice cream, cold cuts, or other snack at this family-run Italian grocery. For more on Terranova's, see p. 64, **7**. *3308 Esplanade Ave.* ☎ *504/482-4131. $.*

A gated tomb at Cypress Grove Cemetery.

Above ground tombs at Lafayette Cemetery No. 1.

⑤ ★★ **Cypress Grove & Greenwood cemeteries.** After Cypress Grove Cemetery opened, bodies of volunteer firefighters were moved here from other cemeteries. Greenwood Cemetery is home to New Orleans's first Civil War memorial. Greenwood is also the final resting place of Pulitzer Prize-winning author John Kennedy Toole, famous for his novel *A Confederacy of Dunces*. See p 14, ⑧. 🕐 *1–2 hr. 5200 Canal Blvd.*

⑥ ★ **Lake Lawn Cemetery.** This is New Orleans' most ornate and youngest cemetery, founded in 1872. It was originally a racetrack; rumor has it that Charles T. Howard, a "new money" Yankee, was turned away, so he exacted revenge by purchasing the property, demolishing the track, and opening this most opulent of graveyards. Howard's tomb is in the middle of the cemetery, along with more notable folks such as bandleader Louis Prima, Popeye's chicken founder Al Copeland, New Orleans district attorney Jim Garrison, and Anne Rice's husband, the poet Stan Rice. 🕐 *90 min. 5100 Pontchartrain Blvd.* ☎ *504/ 486-6331. www.lakelawnmetairie. com. Free admission. Daily 9am– 4pm. Closed holidays.*

Take bus route no. 27 Louisiana to the Garden District, exit at St. Charles and Louisiana avenues, go 5 blocks east then turn south on Washington Avenue.

⑦ ★★ **Lafayette Cemetery No. 1.** See p 17, ④. 🕐 *1 hr. Entrance gate 1400 block Washington Ave.*

A sculpture in Lafayette Cemetery No. 1.

History Buffs

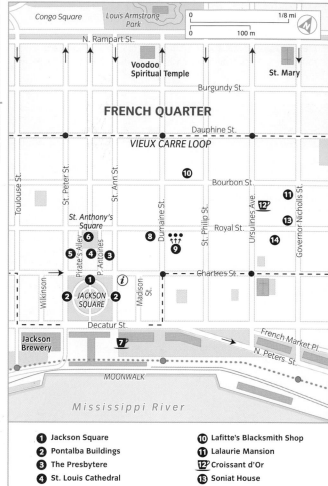

1 Jackson Square
2 Pontalba Buildings
3 The Presbytere
4 St. Louis Cathedral
5 The Cabildo
6 The Creole House and
   the Jackson House
7 Café du Monde
8 Madame John's Legacy
9 Miltenberger Houses
   (900 Royal St., 906 Royal St.,
   and 910 Royal St.)

10 Lafitte's Blacksmith Shop
11 Lalaurie Mansion
12 Croissant d'Or
13 Soniat House
14 Old Ursuline Convent

i Information
••●•• Riverwalk streetcar
        route/stops
--●-- Vieux Carre loop
        route/stops

It could be argued that the entire city of New Orleans—
which predates the founding of the U.S.A.—merits a spot on the
National Register of Historic Places. But if your vacation days are limited (and you can tear yourself away from the History Channel long
enough), the French Quarter is rich with 18th- and 19th-century landmarks that have miraculously survived fires, floods, hurricanes, and
modern development. **START: Jackson Square, bordered by St. Peter,
Chartres, St. Ann, and Decatur streets.**

❶ Jackson Square. Historically,
Jackson Square has been a bustling
social gathering place where you
can shop, eat, and people-watch. See
p 9, **❷**. ⏲ *20 min. Bounded by Decatur, St. Ann, Chartres, and St. Peter
sts. Free admission.*

❷ Pontalba Buildings. These
striking, red-brick residences were
constructed from 1849 to 1851 and
were originally retail shops on the
first floor and 16 high-end homes on
the upper two and a half floors. (The
half-floor attics were designated as
the servants' quarters.) The ornamen-
tal ironwork inspired an architectural
trend that can be seen throughout
the Vieux Carré (French Quarter). It's
a wonder that the residences were
built at all. The developer, the Baroness Micaela Almonester de Pontalba,
survived family feuding, divorce, and
bullet wounds *before* embarking on

this ambitious project, and tempestu-
ous relationships with multiple archi-
tects and contractors *during* the
entire process. After the Civil War,
the respectable tenants began to
move out. By 1900, the homes had
been divided into apartments
crowded with the poor living in slum
conditions. Despite restoration, most
of the homes remain cut up into
apartments, probably because they
are in such demand. The Louisiana
State Museum maintains one completely restored home, known as the
1850 House (523 St. Ann St.), which is
open to the public. ⏲ *20 min. St. Ann
and St. Peter sts. facing Jackson
Square.* ☎ *800/568-6968. http://lsm.
crt.state.la.us. 1850 House admission
$3 adults, $2 students/seniors, free
children 11 and under. Tues–Sun
9am–5pm.*

Painters, among other artists, line Jackson square.

One of the Pontalba buildings on Jackson Square.

❸ The Presbytere. Originally known as the Casa Curial (Ecclesiastical House), the Presbytere got its name from the residence, or presbytery, for the Capuchin monks that burned down on the site. It was built in 1791 as a twin of the Cabildo, or Town Hall, to the left of the cathedral. First it was used commercially, then it served as a courthouse until 1911, when it fell into the hands of the Louisiana State Museum. If your visit doesn't coincide with the Carnival season, you can get a taste of the revelry through the Presbytere's year-round Mardi Gras exhibit. The collection of ornate costumes and masks, rare artifacts, "royal baubles," music, and videos tell the story behind the holiday from its humble

Elaborate Mardi Gras costumes on display at the Presbytere.

origins to its famous reputation today as the world's biggest free show.
🕐 *1 hr. 751 Chartres St.* 📞 *800/568-6968. http://lsm.crt.state.la.us. Admission $6 adults, $5 students/seniors, free children 12 and under. Tues–Sun 9am–5pm.*

❹ St. Louis Cathedral. An iconic image of New Orleans, the 280-year-old church boasts ornate architectural decor, including stained-glass windows and a massive mural. See p 9, ❸. 🕐 *20 min. 615 Pere Antoine Alley (on Jackson Square).*

❺ The Cabildo. The museum offers educational exhibits about early Louisiana history and culture, including mourning and burial customs, and the changing roles of women in the South. See p 10, ❹. 🕐 *45 min. 701 Chartres St.*

❻ The Creole House and the Jackson House. Architecturally, these homes fit right in with antebellum French Quarter residences and now house administrative offices for the Friends of the Cabildo. However, the site itself has seen quite a few changes over the past 3 centuries. In the early 19th century, there was a French guard house behind the *corps de garde,* or police station, where the Cabildo now sits. In 1769, during Spanish colonial times, a *calabozo,* or prison, replaced the guard house, though it, too, was eventually demolished in 1837. 🕐 *10 min. 616 Pirates Alley and 619 Pirates Alley.* ☎ *800/568-6968 or 504/568-6968. http://lsm.crt.state.la.us. No public admission.*

7 ★★★ kids Café du Monde. Fuel up on strong café au lait (chicory coffee with milk) and delicious, melt-in-your-mouth beignets (pronounced ben-yays), fried doughnuts generously coated in powdered sugar. New Orleans' "original French Market coffee stand" started serving customers in 1862. *800 Decatur St.* ☎ *504/528-9933. $.*

8 Madame John's Legacy. The French Colonial style seems more in keeping with a plantation home on the bayou, but this simple, two-story dwelling that sharply contrasts with its tall, elegant townhouse neighbors is a survivor. Built in 1788 just after the great fire of that year, it is the second-oldest building in the Quarter after the Old Ursuline Convent. In fact, it is one of the few remaining examples of Creole buildings in the entire

You can't go wrong with a plate of beignets and a cup of chicory coffee at the Café du Monde.

Mississippi Valley. The curious name alludes to a title character in New Orleans writer George Washington Cable's short story, "Tite Poulette." Madame John was a quadroon (someone of one-quarter African ancestry) whose late lover willed this house to her. The Louisiana State Museum acquired the property and furnished the home with period pieces. 🕐 *30 min. 632 Dumaine St.* ☎ *800/568-6968 or 504/568-6968. http://lsm.crt.state. la.us. Free admission. Tues–Sun 9am–5pm.*

9 Miltenberger Houses. Back in the day, it wasn't unusual for wealthy families to build homes for

The Presbytere, below, and the Cabildo have nearly identicals facades.

Madame John's Legacy.

their offspring. However, it's impressive that in 1838, widow and single mother Aimée Miltenberger managed to construct three separate residences, one for each of her sons, at a total cost of $29,176. The walls were made of imported red brick and the design—while mostly Creole—shows some Greek Revival influence, which was trendy at the time. For example, the staircase is indoors. Be sure to note the oak leaves with acorns in the cast-iron details, a symbol of food and shelter, and health and hospitality. ⏱ *10 min. 900 Royal St., 906 Royal St., and 910 Royal St. No public admission.*

⑩ Lafitte's Blacksmith Shop.

Natives of New Orleans cringe at the thought of the Quarter becoming "Disneyfied," that is, prettied up so it looks like a pristine amusement park rather than real living

Lafitte's Blacksmith Shop, a popular French Quarter watering hole.

history, with all of its quaint charms. The blacksmith shop's current, gaudy look was a compromised "restoration" in response to criticism from the Vieux Carré Commission that the building was neglected. Now its halfhearted stucco job—allowing a few glimpses of the intriguing "brick-between-post" design—barely resembles the worn, but more realistic image that is still found on postcards and in books, making tourists wonder if it's even the same structure. Hard to believe that this is supposedly the oldest building in the Mississippi Valley, dating back to at least 1722. Named for infamous pirate Jean Lafitte, it attracted the literary likes of Tennessee Williams. ⏱ *15 min. 941 Bourbon St. ☎ 504/593-9761. Free admission. Open daily 11am–closing.*

⑪ The Lalaurie Mansion. This

is believed to be the most haunted house in the Quarter, which might be the reason why actor Nicolas Cage bought it in 2007. In the early 1800s, a well-to-do Creole couple, Dr. Louis and Delphine Lalaurie, resided here with a houseful of slaves. Delphine was known for extravagant parties, so when she was seen chasing a slave girl onto the roof who then fell to her death, neighbors chose to mind their own business. When a fire broke out in 1834, it was discovered that Madame Lalaurie had been slowly torturing to death some of her slaves, who were hidden away in secret rooms. Supposedly the cook, who was chained to her stove, started the fire, choosing death over her hell-on-earth existence. The Lalauries fled an angry mob and moved to Paris, never to be seen in New Orleans again. The home was restored, but subsequent occupants didn't stay long because they

The courtyard at the Old Ursuline Convent.

reported chilling screams and moans, strange occurrences, and, for a lucky few, ghost sightings. ⏱ *5 min. 1140 Royal St. No public admission.*

12 Croissant d'Or. At the turn of the 20th century, this used to be Angelo Brocato's bakery (which relocated to Mid-City) with separate entrances for men and women. (You can still see the old LADIES ENTRANCE sign on the sidewalk.) The display case is filled with goodies, everything from chocolate and fruit-filled golden, flaky croissants to ham-and-cheese quiches. If you have a hard time choosing, keep in mind that the prices are cheap, so you can afford to pick a plateful, though the extra calories might cost you. Opt for a seat beside the decrepit fountain in the courtyard and toss a few crumbs to the friendly sparrows. *617 Ursulines St.* ☎ *504/524-4663. $.*

13 Soniat House. Newly restored in 2005, what is now a hotel was once the upscale Creole residence of wealthy plantation owner Joseph Soniat Dufossat. His father, chevalier Guy Saunhac du Fossat, was sent to Louisiana by Louis XV in 1751 to help the colonial governor defend against Native American attacks. Joseph built the house in 1829 and raised his family there until his death in 1852. By the time his wife died in 1865, the Quarter was no longer fashionable among aristocrats and the house passed from owner to owner who cared little for its noble roots. In 1945, pioneering preservationists restored the home, and in 1983, it opened its doors as a hotel. The owners adored early-19th-century architecture and art and decorated the house with period furnishings. See p 146. ⏱ *10 min. 1133 Chartres St. Free admission. Open daily.*

14 Old Ursuline Convent. Once home to the first girls-only school in the United States, the convent serves as a museum for local Catholic history dating back to 1718. ⏱ *40 min. See p. 10, 7. 1100–1116 Chartres St.*

The old Angelo Brocato's sign outside the Croissant D'or.

New Orleans Literati

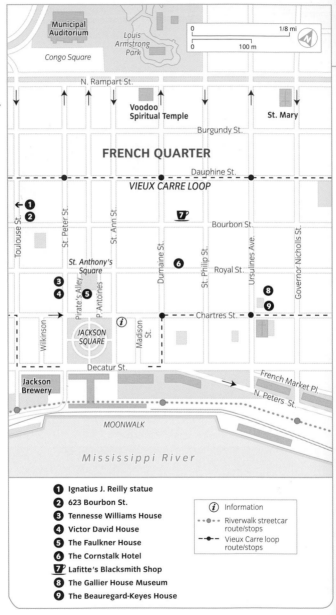

1. Ignatius J. Reilly statue
2. 623 Bourbon St.
3. Tennesse Williams House
4. Victor David House
5. The Faulkner House
6. The Cornstalk Hotel
7. Lafitte's Blacksmith Shop
8. The Gallier House Museum
9. The Beauregard-Keyes House

ⓘ Information

•••• Riverwalk streetcar route/stops

—•— Vieux Carre loop route/stops

If they weren't lucky enough to be born here, writers from William Faulkner to Richard Ford to Tennessee Williams have been drawn to New Orleans for its colorful history, eccentric characters, and sensual charms. Apparently, for writers, the city's contrasts—beauty and decay, rich and poor—kick start the imagination.
START: **Victor David House, 620 St. Peter St.**

❶ Ignatius J. Reilly statue.
At the Canal Street entrance to the Chateau Bourbon Hotel (see p. 140), stands a likeness of Ignatius J. Reilly, the hero of John Kennedy O'Toole's novel *A Confederacy of Dunces*. The clock, under which we first meet Reilly, is now in the hotel's Clock Bar. *800 Iberville St.*

❷ 623 Bourbon St. Truman Capote and Tennessee Williams both lived in this house (not at the same time). It's

A plaque commemorates the Victor David House.

VICTOR DAVID HOUSE

ERECTED IN 1839
FOR VICTOR DAVID, A NATIVE OF
GASCONY, FRANCE, AND
HIS WIFE ANN RABASSA
DAVID SIGLE AND SAMUEL STEWART, BUILDERS

PURCHASED AND RESTORED IN 1925
AS ITS CLUBHOUSE BY
LE PETIT SALON
A LADIES' LITERARY GROUP
ONE OF THE FIRST TO RECOGNIZE AND PRESERVE
THE CULTURAL TRADITIONS OF THE VIEUX CARRÉ

THIS PLAQUE DEDICATED ON APRIL 28, 1989

now owned by Lindy Boggs, local political figure and mother of national news personality Cokie Roberts. *623 Bourbon St.*

❸ Tennesse Williams House. If any writer has ever captured the spirit of New Orleans, it's got to be Tennessee Williams in his iconic work "A Streetcar Named Desire." From his attic room at 632 St. Peter's St., he wrote the play in 1946. It is from this residence that he heard "that rattle trap streetcar named Desire running along Royal and the one named Cemeteries running along Canal and it seemed the perfect metaphor for the human condition." *632 St. Peter's St.*

❹ Victor David House. In 1838, wealthy merchant Victor David built this exquisite example of sophisticated Greek Revival styling to show off his family's social standing. Nearly a century later, historian-novelist Grace King purchased the property to serve as headquarters for Le Petit Salon, of which she was president. The ladies' club was organized in 1924 in order to preserve New Orleans's, and in particular, the French Quarter's culture. 🕐 *10 min. 620 St. Peter St. No public admission.*

Victor David House.

Books by William Faulkner on sale at Faulkner House Books.

James; a tour can be arranged in advance for a donation to their non-profit organization, the Pirate's Alley Faulkner Society, Inc. Together with retired English professor Kenneth W. Holditch, the couple founded the Society to assist writers and host events throughout the year, including the annual Words & Music arts festival in the Fall. 🕐 *30 min. 624 Pirate's Alley.* ☎ *504/586-1609 or 504/525-5615. Bookstore:* ☎ *504/ 524-2940. www.faulknerhouse books.net or www.wordsandmusic. org. Free admission. Bookstore daily 10am–5:30pm. Closed Mardi Gras.*

❻ The Cornstalk Hotel. Author Harriet Beecher Stowe is believed to have stayed here while researching the slave markets, which she featured in her famous anti-slavery novel *Uncle Tom's Cabin.* See p 52, **❺**. 🕐 *15 min. 915 Royal St. Free admission. Open daily.*

❼ ★★ Lafitte's Blacksmith Shop. Tennessee Williams liked to hang out here. With the candlelit bar, exposed antique brick, and rumored ghosts, it certainly invites creative musing. Order up your favorite drink and see where your mind takes you. See p 120. *941 Bourbon St.* ☎ *504/522-9377. $.*

❺ ★★★ The Faulkner House. From the 1920s to the 1950s, the Vieux Carré was known as the "Greenwich Village of the South" for its steady influx of artists and writers attracted to the Quarter's decadent ways. Nobel Laureate William Faulkner was one of the "bohemian literati," arriving in 1925 and renting a ground-floor apartment in this property. During his short, 1-year stay, he wrote his debut novel, *Soldiers' Pay.* Current owners Joseph DeSalvo, Jr., and Rosemary James painstakingly restored the Greek Revival–style Creole town house, built around 1840, which has since been named a national literary landmark. The ground floor is **Faulkner House Books,** where you can find a marvelous collection of Southern literature. The upper floors are private quarters for DeSalvo and

❽ The Gallier House Museum. Designed and lived in by prolific local architect James Gallier in the mid-1800s, it's allegedly the inspiration for vampires Lestat and Louis's home in Anne Rice's *Interview with the Vampire.* When constructed in 1857, the house was ahead of its time, featuring hot and cold running water, an indoor bathroom, and indoor kitchen. 🕐 *45 min. 1132 Royal St.* ☎ *504/525-5661. www. hgghh.org. Admission $10 adults, $8*

More Than Vampires

Anne Rice is New Orleans' most famous native writer (and richest, too, earning $7-million-plus per book). But you're selling yourself short if you don't check out Pulitzer Prize–winning classics like John Kennedy Toole's *A Confederacy of Dunces* and Shirley Ann Grau's *The Keepers of the House.* The city's eccentric bluebloods are chronicled in Nancy Lemann's novel, *Lives of the Saints.* If you plan to tour bayou country (see Lafitte in chapter 10), first pry open John Biguenet's *Oyster.* Uptown and the Audubon Zoo are the setting for Valerie Martin's *The Great Divorce,* in which a veterinarian faces the collapse of her marriage and the increasing divide between nature and man. For more suggestions, browse *The Booklover's Guide to New Orleans,* by *Times-Picayune* book editor Susan Larson.

Writer Anne Rice's former home in the Garden District.

seniors and children 8–18, free children 7 and under. Tours Thurs–Fri at 10am, 11am, noon, 2pm, and 3pm; Sat at noon, 1pm, 2pm, and 3pm.

9 ★★ **Beauregard-Keyes House & Garden.** See p 11, **8**.
🕐 *30 min. 1113 Chartres St.*

Mardi Gras

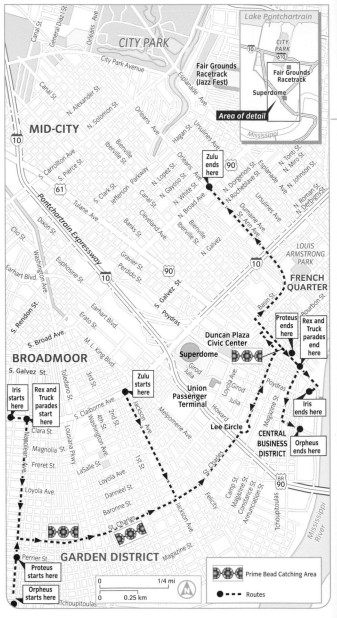

Lake Pontchartrain

CITY PARK

Fair Grounds Racetrack (Jazz Fest)

Area of detail

MID-CITY

Pontchartrain Expressway

Zulu ends here

LOUIS ARMSTRONG PARK

FRENCH QUARTER

BROADMOOR

Zulu starts here

Duncan Plaza Civic Center

Superdome

Union Passenger Terminal

Lee Circle

Proteus ends here

Rex and Truck parades end here

Iris ends here

CENTRAL BUSINESS DISTRICT

Orpheus ends here

Iris starts here

Rex and Truck parades start here

St. Charles

GARDEN DISTRICT

Magazine St.

Proteus starts here

Orpheus starts here

Mississippi River

Prime Bead Catching Area

Routes

0   1/4 mi

0   0.25 km

Mardi Gras—the biggest free party thrown in North America—always falls 46 days before Easter and is the city's most popular attraction. People love the crowds, costumes, and camaraderie; I don't know of another place or time where you can make so many friends just standing on a curb calling out for beads. Below are recommended parades for Lundi Gras (Mon) and Mardi Gras (Tues); citywide parades roll nearly every day in the 2 weeks prior to Mardi Gras day. **START: If you like raucous crowds, join the street party in the French Quarter, especially on Bourbon Street between the 500 and 1000 blocks. If you prefer a little more space, take a cab uptown near Napoleon Avenue.**

A float from the Zulu Aid and Pleasure Club.

Lundi Gras Parades

❶ **Proteus.** The second-oldest Carnival krewe (Mardi Gras society) dates back to 1882 and is comprised of 275 men riding on about 20 old-fashioned floats that still use the original chassis from the 1880s. Throws include (plastic) pearls, lighted beads, flasks, and plush fish. *www.kreweofproteus.com. Starts uptown at Perrier St. and Napoleon Ave., turns east on St. Charles Ave., turns north on Canal St., makes a U-turn at Baronne St., and finishes at Canal and Chartres sts. Free admission. Lundi Gras (Mon). Begins 5:15pm.*

❷ ★★★ **Orpheus.** Native New Orleanian Harry Connick, Jr.'s, young superkrewe is less than 20 years old but boasts some of the most popular megafloats, including

Find a Parade

Arthur Hardy's Mardi Gras Guide is an annual magazine and my personal Mardi Gras bible come Twelfth Night. It contains the all-important parade schedule, calendar of related events, and informative articles on Carnival history. You can buy one almost anywhere in the city—including bookstores, drug stores, and grocery stores (it usually comes out right after Christmas). You can also order a copy by phone ☎ **504/913-1563,** or online at www. arthurhardy.com.

A brass band leads revelers through the French Quarter on Mardi Gras Day.

the Leviathan and Trojan Horse. More than 1,200 men and women on 30 floats throw beads, pearls, silver doubloons, plush ducks, go-cups, and more. Celebrity guests serve as "royalty"; past guest monarchs include Whoopi Goldberg, Glenn Close, Sandra Bullock, Stevie Wonder, Quincy Jones, Laurence Fishburne, Vanessa Williams, Dan Aykroyd, James Brown, Little Richard, David Copperfield, Josh Hartnett, Anne Rice, Dominic Monaghan, and Brad Paisley. *www.kreweof orpheus.net. Starts uptown at Tchoupitoulas and Magazine sts. and ends downtown at the Convention Center. Free admission. Lundi Gras (Mon). Begins 6pm.*

Mardi Gras Parades

❸ ★★ **Zulu.** Carnival's premier African-American parade was originally created as a parody of exclusive, haughty Rex before segregation ended; both krewes now allow anyone to join. As the 35 floats and 1,200 riders pass by, keep an eye out for the prized Zulu coconut, a hand-painted souvenir that even the natives scramble for. Hang out near the cops keeping the crowds in check; Zulu members typically pass coconuts to them as thanks. Coconuts used to be thrown like beads, but must now be passed by hand for safety reasons. *www.kreweofzulu. com. Starts uptown at Jackson and St. Charles aves. and ends at Orleans Ave. and N. Broad St. Free admission. Mardi Gras (Tues). Begins 8am.*

❹ ★★ **Rex.** The oldest parade debuted in 1872 and now has more than 600 men riding 27 floats. The royal costumes are a sight to behold—lots of gold and glitter. The throws are fairly traditional, including beads, pearls, doubloons, and go-cups. *www.rexorganization.com. Starts uptown at S. Claiborne and Napoleon aves. and ends downtown*

Be sure to bring a costume if you plan on visiting New Orleans for Mardi Gras.

A crowd pleading and competing for "throws" from a passing float.

at Canal and St. Peter sts. Free admission. Mardi Gras (Tues). Begins 10am.

5 ★ **kids** **Truck parades.** Some parade watchers go home after the "official" end of Mardi Gras with the passing of Rex, but if you want more throws or just want the party to last, hang out to watch more than 200 themed truck floats decorated and ridden by family members. Kids often ride, too, and tend to throw stuffed animals and other cute trinkets to kids waving from the neutral ground or sidewalk. *Starts uptown at S. Claiborne and Napoleon aves. and ends downtown at Canal and St. Peter sts. Free admission. Follows Rex.*

Beads Beget Beads

Want plenty of parade throws? At the very least, wear some "pearls" to the parade. Better yet, wear a costume and yell "Throw me something, mister!" to show some Mardi Gras spirit. It's a given that float riders will always throw beads and stuffed animals to the kids on ladders; they're adorable and they stand out above the crowd, so if you're in the vicinity, you're guaranteed a neck full of beads, too. If you and a neighboring reveler catch the same bunch of beads, it's common courtesy to share the strands.

Jazz History: Where the Greats Got Their Starts

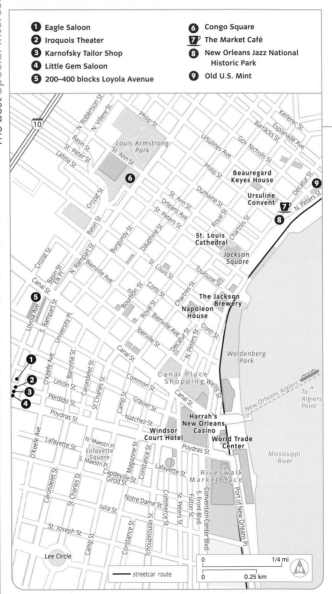

1. Eagle Saloon
2. Iroquois Theater
3. Karnofsky Tailor Shop
4. Little Gem Saloon
5. 200–400 blocks Loyola Avenue
6. Congo Square
7. The Market Café
8. New Orleans Jazz National Historic Park
9. Old U.S. Mint

Many of Jazz music's greatest legends came from New Orleans. Walk along a few blocks of S. Rampart St., and you'll see the origins of some of New Orleans's most beloved and revered musicians. Stroll the French Quarter and you'll hear Jazz wafting out the doorway of many a nightclub, bar, or retail store. This tour takes you through a section once known as the "Back of Town," along S. Rampart Street, which birthed such talents as Buddy Bolden, Louis Armstrong, and Jelly Roll Morton. Though some of the establishments on the tour below are closed and don't allow visitors, we still recommend taking a stroll through the neighborhoods where Jazz originated and planted its still strong roots. START: **Take a cab to S. Rampart Street.**

❶ Eagle Saloon. Though it's in disrepair now, hopes run high (and progress is being made) for eventually turning this dilapidated establishment into the New Orleans Music Hall of Fame. Jazz masters including Louis Armstrong, Buddy Bolden, Jelly Roll Morton, and King Oliver all played this dearly loved club that the Smithsonian recently called the "birthplace of American Jazz music." One of three Jazz-related venues in the building, the Eagle Saloon was a place for big names to relax between gigs at the Odd Fellows Hall and Masonic Hall next door. *401 S. Rampart St.*

❷ Iroquois Theater. Many Jazz musicians got their starts here by accompanying silent films and stage acts with Jazz and Blues music. A young Louis Armstrong is said to have won a talent contest here. *413–415 S. Rampart St.*

❸ Karnofsky Tailor Shop. As a boy, Louis Armstrong worked here for the Karnofsky family. They took a shine to Louis and are rumored to have given him an advance on his pay so that he could buy a cornet. Needless to say, their generosity paid off. Armstrong remained close to the family throughout his long career. The shop is listed in the National Register of Historic Places. *427–431 S. Rampart St.*

❹ Little Gem Saloon. After suffering from neglect and dilapidation along with the other establishments listed above, the Little Gem Saloon is now being renovated and will reopen as a retail, office, and apartment-living space. This building

Harry Connick, Jr. and Branford Marsalis take the stage at Jazz Fest.

Maison Bourbon in the French Quarter, an oasis of Jazz in the Bourbon Street storm.

once housed a nightclub called Pete's Blue Heaven, where the Zulu Social Aid and Pleasure Club frequently started and ended its Jazz funerals. *445 S. Rampart St.*

5 200–400 blocks of Loyola Avenue. Jelly Roll Morton and Louis Armstrong once lived along this section of Loyola Avenue. Also located here was Funky Butt Hall (formally known as Union Sons Hall) where Buddy Bolden would thrill the crowds with his one-of-a-kind cornet playing. These blocks now make-up the New Orleans Civic Center. *200–400 blocks of Loyola Avenue.*

6 Congo Square. In the mid-1800s to early 1900s slaves were allowed to gather in the square on Sundays for singing, dancing, and playing instruments (drums, in particular). Many musicians and musical styles grew from this cultural phenomenon. *In Louis Armstrong Park. N. Rampart Street between Toulouse and St. Phillip streets, facing the French Quarter.*

7 The Market Café. Coffee drinks, po'boys, salads, and cocktails should satisfy any hunger or thirst in your party. *1000 Decatur St.* ☎ *504/527-5000. $.*

8 ★★ New Orleans Jazz National Historical Park. The NOJNHP offers Ranger-lead walks, as well as providing self-guided walking tours, with opportunities to learn about New Orleans native Jazz music and musicians. You can download the tours online or stop by the visitors center for a map. Documentaries and live music are also frequently on hand. Be sure to ask about what's on tap while you're in town. The Oral History Project is a wonderful living document of New Orleans culture. Video-taped oral histories are available on more than 100 New Orleans legends (musical and otherwise) including Dooky Chase, Tuba Fats Lacen, Moon Landrieu, Willie Metcalf, Jr., and Babette Ory. The NOJNHP is in the process of moving and making

Jazz Clubs

Don't miss out on hearing the best Jazz around town. For complete reviews of these and other night spots, turn to our Nightlife chapter, on p. 109.

Maison Bourbon (p 121), 641 Bourbon St.
Palm Court Jazz Café (p 121), 1204 Decatur St.
Sweet Lorraine's (p 120), 1931 St. Claude Ave.
Preservation Hall (p 121), 726 St. Peter St.

Jazz Fest: Laissez les bon temps roulez!

What started as a local festival of Jazz musicians has now become a worldwide phenomenon featuring performances by the likes of Bruce Springsteen, Stevie Wonder, Bob Dylan, and Wynton Marsalis. The nearly week-long **New Orleans Jazz & Heritage Festival** (the event's official name) is held at the Fair Grounds Race Course and celebrates the spirit and musical heritage of New Orleans. When the festival started it took place in Congo Square (see ❻, below) and attracted only a few hundred attendees. The festival now plays host to hundreds of thousands of fans, so it's imperative to make your plans way ahead of time. Hotels, restaurant reservations, and flights can fill up months in advance. If possible book up to a year out. You won't know who's on the bill yet, but you pretty much can't go wrong. Whether you're listening to an adored local blues band from the Delta or cheering on Harry Connick, Jr. or Dave Matthews, you're sure to have a big time. For information contact the New Orleans Jazz & Heritage Festival, 1205 N. Rampart St. ☎ 504/410-4100; www.nojazzfest.com).

Armstrong Park their permanent home. *Visitors Center: 916 N. Peters St. ☎ 504/589-4841. 9am–5pm Tues–Sat. Closed holidays. Headquarters: 419 Decatur St. ☎ 504/589-4806. Mon–Fri 8am–4:30pm. Closed holidays. www.nps.gov/jazz/.*

Sweet Lorraine's.

❾ **Old U.S. Mint.** The Old U.S. Mint holds the sizeable Louisiana State University Jazz Collection. In addition to such treasures as Louis Armstrong's cornet and bugle and Kid Ory's trombone, the exhibit holds tens of thousands of recordings, photographs, copies of sheet music, posters, and other Jazz memorabilia. Though only a small amount (less than 1%) of the collection was damaged due to Hurricane Katrina and its aftermath, most of it was quickly refurbished. However, the Mint still remains closed. Call before your visit, in hopes that it will have reopened by then. *400 Esplanade Ave. ☎ 504/568-6968. http://lsm.crt.state.la.us/mintex.htm/. Currently open by appointment only for researchers.*

The Best Museums

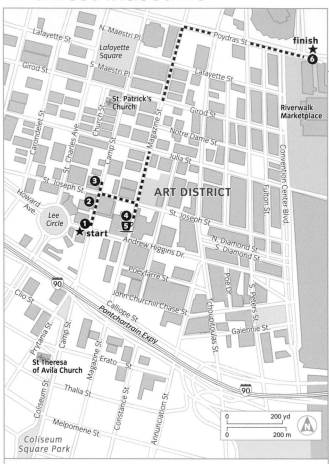

1. **Civil War Museum at Confederate Memorial Hall**
2. **The Ogden Museum of Southern Art**
3. **Contemporary Arts Center**
4. **National World War II Museum**
5. **PJ's Coffee & Tea**
6. **Southern Food and Beverage Museum & Museum of the American Cocktail**

Today's vibrant Arts District was once a shabby industrial area of abandoned warehouses. Thanks to adaptive reuse, these rundown buildings have been transformed into spacious galleries showcasing Southern art, history, and heritage. They have given new life—and unified purpose—to an old neighborhood. **START: Take the St. Charles Streetcar to Lee Circle and walk 1 block south to Camp Street.**

A display of uniforms at the Civil War Museum at Confederate Memorial Hall.

❶ Civil War Museum at Confederate Memorial Hall. The oldest museum in Louisiana is absolutely worth a visit. Its Civil War memorabilia includes uniforms, photographs, guns, battle flags, swords, and personal belongings of General Robert E. Lee, General P. G. T. Beauregard, and Confederate president Jefferson Davis. ⏱ ½–1 hr. *929 Camp St.* ☎ *504/523-4522. www. confederatemuseum.com. Admission $5 adults, $4 students/seniors, $2 children 11 and under. Thurs–Sat 10am–4pm.*

❷ ★★ Ogden Museum of Southern Art. Affiliated with the University of New Orleans, this young museum's permanent and rotating exhibitions are dedicated to Southern art in a variety of mediums—from clay and glass to paintings and photography—by self-taught and classically trained artists from 1890 to today. The sleek modern building alone is a soaring, inspiring space featuring a glass facade and "floating" staircase. ⏱ 1–2 hr. *925 Camp St.* ☎ *504/539-9600. www.ogden museum.org. Admission $10 adults, $8 students/seniors, $5 children 5–17, free children 4 and under. Wed–Sun 10am–5pm, live music Thurs 6–9pm.*

❸ Contemporary Arts Center. Modern art fans gather here to socialize and appreciate experimental plays, dance productions, concerts, and the occasional comedy and film screening. After walking

Live music is on-hand at the Ogden's annual White Linen Party.

through 10,000 square feet (929 sq. m) of gallery exhibits, unwind at the Cyber Bar & Café. 🕐 *1 hr. 900 Camp St.* ☎ *504/528-3800. www.cacno. org. Tickets $5 adults, $3 students/ seniors, free children 15 and under. Thurs–Sun 11am–4pm.*

④ ★★★ National World War II Museum. A cavernous old warehouse has been transformed into an extraordinary tribute to the "Greatest Generation." The museum humanizes the soldiers no matter which side they fought on. My grandfather, a World War II veteran, spent 6 hours perusing the exhibits and artifacts, watching short documentaries, and talking to fellow veterans. 🕐 *2–3 hr. 945 Magazine St.* ☎ *504/527-6012. www.ddaymuseum.org. Admission $14 adults, $8 students/seniors, $6 children 5–12, free children 4 and under. Daily 9am–5pm.*

5 ★ kids PJ's Coffee & Tea. Order a large iced coffee made with in-house cold-drip Viennese Blend and a hint of Melipone

vanilla, stirred with milk and served over ice. You won't find a better iced coffee anywhere. Sandwiches and pastries are also good. *945 Magazine St.* ☎ *504/ 525-0522. $.*

⑥ Southern Food and Beverage Museum & Museum of the American Cocktail. Newly opened in 2008, SOFAB documents the history of the area's famous foods and drinks. Rotating exhibits cover a wide spectrum of topics ranging from White House cuisine to the history of greens (kale, collards, and the like) so often synonymous with Southern food. The Museum of the American Cocktail tells its own saucy story through artifacts, photos, and special exhibits dedicated to all types of spirits. 🕐 *1–2 hr. 1 Poydras St. (in the Riverwalk Marketplace Mall).* ☎ *504/569-0405. www.southernfood.org and www. museumoftheamericancocktail.org. Admission adults $10, seniors and students $5. Mon–Sat 10am–7pm, Sun noon–6pm.* ●

The National World War II Museum.

The Upper French Quarter

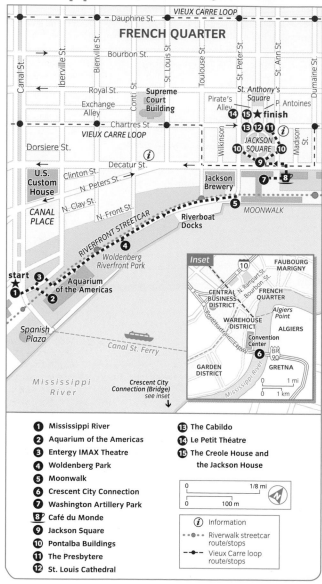

- **1** Mississippi River
- **2** Aquarium of the Americas
- **3** Entergy IMAX Theatre
- **4** Woldenberg Park
- **5** Moonwalk
- **6** Crescent City Connection
- **7** Washington Artillery Park
- **8** Café du Monde
- **9** Jackson Square
- **10** Pontalba Buildings
- **11** The Presbytere
- **12** St. Louis Cathedral
- **13** The Cabildo
- **14** Le Petit Théatre
- **15** The Creole House and the Jackson House

| 0 | 1/8 mi |
| 0 | 100 m |

(i) Information

•••• Riverwalk streetcar route/stops

—•— Vieux Carre loop route/stops

Previous page: Iron-work balconies of the Miltenberger House.

The French Quarter is the lifeblood of New Orleans. Founded in 1718, the Vieux Carré (or Old Square, what we now call the French Quarter) comprised the original city of New Orleans. It burned twice—first in 1788, then again in 1794—and rebuilding took place during Spanish rule, which explains why much of the architecture reflects Spanish influence. The entire French Quarter is only 6 blocks wide by 13 blocks long, bordered by North Rampart Street, Esplanade Avenue, Canal Street, and the Mississippi River. The Upper Quarter is bounded by North Rampart, Orleans Street, Canal Street, and the Mississippi River. Hotels and souvenir shops dominate this area, so you'll find it to be busy and commercial, but many of the Vieux Carre's gems still anchor the neighborhood.
START: **Canal Street at the Mississippi River.**

❶ Mississippi River. Stroll along the parklike east bank of the second longest river in North America, the reason for New Orleans' existence. At this point, the mighty waterway measures 1 mile (1.6km) across and 200 feet (60m) deep in contrast to the tiny 3-foot-deep (.9m) stream at its origin. *At the end of Canal St.*

❷ kids Aquarium of the Americas. One of the top five aquariums in the country features

The Aquarium of the Americas is a great place to cool off and learn with the kids.

an enormous tank with a walk-through tunnel from which you can view sea creatures on both sides and overhead, plus a tropical rainforest complete with waterfalls. Kids can pet baby sharks, see Spots the white alligator, and watch giant channel catfish. ⏱ *1–2 hr. 1 Canal St.* ☎ *800/774-7394 or 504/581-4629. www.auduboninstitute.org. Admission $18 adults, $14 seniors, $11 children 2–12. Tues–Sun 10am–5pm.*

❸ kids Entergy IMAX Theatre. Large-screen 3-D documentaries on everything from dinosaurs to the Rolling Stones (was that redundant?) entertain kids of all ages. Be sure to inquire about aquarium/IMAX combination admission. ⏱ *1–2 hr. Next door to the aquarium.* ☎ *800/774-7394 or 504/581-4629. www. auduboninstitute.org. Imax only tickets: $9 adults, $8 seniors, $6 children 2–12. Tues–Sun 10am–5pm.*

❹ Woldenberg Park. Wander through nearly 20 acres (8 hectares) of open space along the riverfront and meditate on the elegant Holocaust Memorial designed by Israeli artist Yaacov Agam, a pioneer of kinetic art. *On the river behind the 500 block of Decatur St.*

Looking over the Mississippi from Washington Artillery Park.

⑤ Moonwalk. This scenic path is named for former New Orleans mayor Maurice Edwin "Moon" Landrieu, father of U.S. Senator Mary Landrieu (D-Louisiana) and Louisiana Lieutenant Governor Mitch Landrieu. Built in the 1970s, the wooden promenade encouraged the public use and appreciation for the riverfront after preservationists struck down a 1960s proposal for an expressway along the river. *Along the Mississippi River, btw. Canal St. and just past Orleans St.*

⑥ Crescent City Connection. The bridge is comprised of two separate steel spans. The first was built from 1954 to 1958 and the second was constructed from 1981 to 1988. It ranks as the fifth most traveled toll bridge in the country, with an annual traffic volume of more than

Entergy IMAX Theatre.

63 million. *Spans the Mississippi River to Algiers Point.*

⑦ Washington Artillery Park. You get postcard-perfect views of Ol' Man River or Jackson Square depending on which direction you face. Sit on the amphitheater steps for people-watching and energetic dancing by tip-hustling street performers. *On Decatur St. next to Café du Monde.*

★★★ kids ⑧ Café du Monde. New Orleans' favorite coffeehouse has been around since 1862, when it debuted as a simple coffee stand in the French Market. It remains popular today among locals and tourists alike for its inexpensive, signature beignets and café au lait. *800 Decatur St.* ☎ *504/528-9933. www. cafedumonde.com. $.*

⑨ Jackson Square. See p 9, ②.

⑩ Pontalba Buildings. Despite an attempt on her life by her father-in-law, in which she was shot in the chest and hands, and the acrimonious divorce that followed, the Baroness Micaela Almonester de Pontalba became a savvy businesswoman and designed and built these exclusive town homes in the 1840s. They remain in great demand today. See p 25, ②.

St. Ann and St. Peter sts. facing Jackson Square.

⓫ The Presbytere. True Mardi Gras fans can't resist the educational (and permanent) exhibit on the city's favorite holiday featured in the Presbytere. We've come a long way from mule-powered floats! See p 26, ❸. *751 Chartres St.*

⓬ St. Louis Cathedral. See p 9, ❸. *615 Pere Antoine Alley (on Jackson Square).*

⓭ The Cabildo. Step inside this national historic landmark and experience the sights, sounds, and stories of the birth of Louisiana, beginning with the Louisiana Purchase in 1803, which drew a crowd to Jackson Square. This is also the site of the infamous 1896 "separate but equal" *Plessy v. Ferguson* decision which was overturned in 1954. *701 Chartres St.* See p. 10, ❹.

⓮ Le Petit Théatre is an early-20th-century, Spanish Colonial building that serves one of the oldest community theater troupes in the country and hosts the annual

The Presbytere houses a Mardi Gras Museum, which is part of the Louisiana State Museum.

Tennessee Williams Literary Festival every spring. See p. 131. *616 St. Peter St.* ☎ *504/522-2081. www. lepetittheatre.com.*

⓯ The Creole House and the Jackson House. See p 26, ❻. *616 Pirates Alley and 619 Pirates Alley.*

A performance at Le Petit Théatre in the French Quarter.

The Lower French Quarter

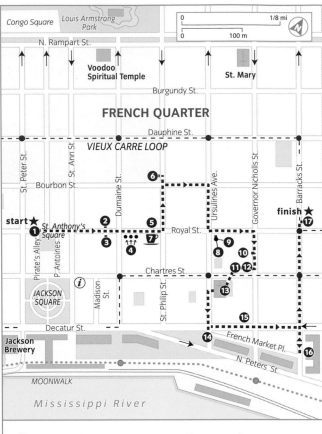

1. 700–800 blocks of Royal Street
2. Dejan House
3. Madame John's Legacy
4. Miltenberger Houses
   (900 Royal St., 906 Royal St., and 910 Royal St.)
5. The Cornstalk Hotel
6. Lafitte's Blacksmith Shop
7. CC's Community Coffee House
8. The Lalaurie Mansion
9. The Gallier House Museum
10. Clay House
11. Beauregard-Keyes House
12. Soniat House
13. Old Ursuline Convent
14. French Market
15. 521 Gov. Nicholls St.
16. Old U.S. Mint
17. Gauche Mansion

i Information

••••• Riverwalk streetcar route/stops

–•– Vieux Carre loop route/stops

The Lower Quarter is geared more toward locals and Quarter residents than tourists. There are far fewer T-shirt and souvenir shops and many more condos, apartments, and single family homes than you'll see in the Upper Quarter. A walk through the Lower Quarter will charm you with unique architecture and a sense of history. START: **Orleans Street at Royal Street.**

① **700–800 blocks of Royal Street.** To walk Royal Street is to be surrounded by fine antiques, estate jewelry, home accessories, vintage paraphernalia, and more. By all means, don't limit yourself to this 2-block stretch if something catches your eye. Whenever I'm down this way, I stop by **Rodrigue Studio** (*721 Royal St.*), featuring Cajun artist George Rodrigue's famous "Blue Dog" paintings, **Bergen Putman Gallery** (*730 Royal St.*), **The Bottom of the Cup Tearoom** (*732 Royal St.*) for a fanciful tea-leaf reading, **Vive La France** (*823 Royal St.*) to smell its luxury imported soaps, and **Hové** (*824 Royal St.*), New Orleans's oldest perfumery. See the "The Best Shopping" chapter (p 73) for more details on individual stores.

② **Dejan House.** The site was first purchased by Jean Baptiste Dejan in 1813, well after the 1788 fire burned down everything on the block. He planned to build an impressive home

Artifacts on display at Madame John's Legacy.

for his family, as befitting a city alderman. But his ideas proved grander than his bank account; he lost the unfinished home to creditors in 1815. When the beautiful Creole town house was complete—from its elegant casement windows to its wrought-iron balcony railing—one of the creditors, merchant Nicholas Girod, purchased it outright. At the turn of the 20th century, when much of the Quarter fell into ruin, the Dejan House was no exception. Thankfully, early Quarter preservationist Lilian

The Dejan House.

Hovey-King acquired the property in 1944 and restored it so that we might still enjoy it today. *824 Royal St.*

3 Madame John's Legacy. See p 27, **8**. *632 Dumaine St.*

4 Miltenberger Houses. See p 27, **9**. *900-906-910 Royal St.*

5 The Cornstalk Hotel. The unusual cornstalk cast-iron fence is one of only two in the city (the other can be found while walking the Garden District tour), although a similar cornstalk fence guards the Dufour-Plasson House in Esplanade Ridge. The owner of the original house on the site commissioned the fence for his homesick Midwestern wife. See p. 32, **6**. *915 Royal St.*

6 Lafitte's Blacksmith Shop. Supposedly, the pirate Jean Lafitte and his brother Pierre posed as blacksmiths but used the shop as a front for illegal activities. See p 120. *941 Bourbon St.*

7 CC's Community Coffee House. This is the South's retort to Starbucks, offering gourmet coffee, pastries, and sandwiches. Enjoy the view of lush balcony gardens across the street and the sound of carriage horses clop-clopping by. *941 Royal St.* ☎ 504/581-6996. $.

8 The Lalaurie Mansion. This place attracts ghost hunters hoping to see or hear paranormal activity around what is rumored to be the most haunted house in the French Quarter. See p 28, **11**. *1140 Royal St.*

9 The Gallier House Museum. The guided tour of this 1857 manse gives you insight into mid-19th-century life in New Orleans and owner-architect James Gallier's forward-thinking designs. See p 33, **8**. *1132 Royal St.*

10 Clay House. John Clay, the brother of American statesman Henry Clay, built this residence in 1828 for his wife. In the 1890s, Saint Frances Xavier Cabrini used it as a schoolhouse before moving to a larger campus at 3400 Esplanade Ave. to care for the large numbers of children orphaned by yellow fever. *618–20 Gov. Nicholls St.*

11 Beauregard-Keyes House & Garden. This lovely raised cottage and formal garden has survived nearly 200 years' worth of multiple owners, the mob, fire, hurricanes, and modern progress. *1113 Chartres St.*

12 Soniat House. Newly restored in 2005, what is now a hotel was once the upscale Creole residence of wealthy plantation owner Joseph

The courtyard at the Beauregard-Keyes House.

A room at the Soniat House.

Soniat Dufossat. See p 146. *1133 Chartres St.*

⓭ Old Ursuline Convent. See p 10, **❼**. *1100-1116 Chartres St.*

⓮ French Market. The bustling market has stood here since the 1700s. Unfortunately, it's now more of a tourist trap (T-shirt anyone?) than anything else. Worth a look if you need some cheap souvenirs. *Decatur and N. Peters sts. from St. Ann to Barracks sts. www.french market.org. Open daily.*

⓯ 521 Gov. Nicholls St. Actors Brad Pitt and Angelina Jolie purchased this stunning 1830's mansion soon after Hurricane Katrina, bringing much-needed hope and awareness to the city. Nearly 8,000 square feet (743 sq. m), it served as Cosimo Matassa's recording studio in the 1950s. All the musical legends of the time—including Fats Domino, Little Richard, Professor Longhair, and Allen Toussaint—recorded here. The house is believed to be haunted by the ghost of Professor Longhair. *521 Gov. Nicholls St.*

⓰ Old U.S. Mint. Originally built in 1835 to mint money for both the United States and the Confederacy, this sturdy Greek Revival building now houses a fascinating jazz exhibit featuring priceless artifacts such as Louis Armstrong's first trumpet. ***Note:*** The Mint is currently closed, but expected to reopen by the time you read this. *400 Esplanade Ave.* ☎ *800/568-6968 or 504/568-6968. http://lsm.crt.state. la.us.*

⓱ Gauche Mansion. Frenchman John Gauche constructed this elegant, perfectly symmetrical two-story stucco home in 1856 at a cost of $11,000 and raised 12 children there. The granite Doric portico makes for an unusually understated entrance. Unlike most of the residences in the Quarter, the ornate ironwork was not added on later and is original to the home. *704 Esplanade Ave. (at Royal St.).*

Typical New Orleans souvenirs for sale at the French Market.

Garden District

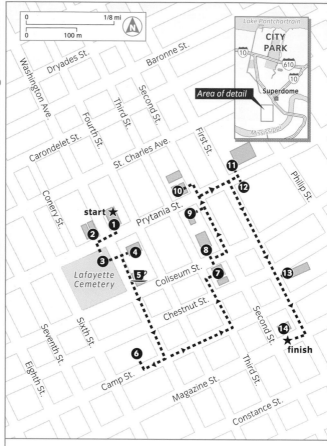

1. The Rink
2. 1500 Washington St.
3. Lafayette Cemetery No. 1
4. Colonel Short's Villa
5. Commander's Palace
6. Former site of Robb Mansion
7. Musson-Bell House
8. Robinson House
9. Davis House
10. Our Lady of Perpetual Help Chapel
11. Bradish Johnson House
12. Toby's Corner
13. Rosegate
14. Payne-Strachan House

Originally part of the city of Lafayette, the Garden District became a fashionable residential area for nouveau riche Americans who were not welcome among established wealthy Creole families in the French Quarter and Esplanade Ridge. Many of the 19th-century mansions have magnificent, perfectly manicured gardens, hence the district's name. This exclusive neighborhood—bordered by Magazine Street and Jackson, St. Charles, and Louisiana avenues—is best experienced via the St. Charles Streetcar and on foot. **START: Corner of Washington and Prytania streets.**

❶ The Rink. Originally an ice skating rink built in 1884, this quaint little shopping center offers a coffee shop, bookstore, and boutiques. *2727 Prytania St.* ☎ *504/899-0335.*

❷ 1500 Washington St. Now a private home, this is the former Behrman Gym where 1892 World Champion fighter "Gentleman Jim" Corbett trained.

❸ Lafayette Cemetery No. 1. Established in 1833 on the former Livaudais Plantation in the city of Lafayette, it's now located in one of New Orleans' most exclusive neighborhoods. Despite its location and small size, it's still unwise to visit alone. Please join a tour group. See p. 17, ❹. *1400 block of Washington Ave.*

❹ Colonel Short's Villa. Before you see the 1859 Italianate manse set back on the property, you'll be captivated by the unusual cornstalk

The renowned Commander's Palace.

cast-iron fence that surrounds it. (Similar fences are found guarding the Cornstalk Hotel in the French Quarter and the Dufour-Plasson House in Esplanade Ridge.) *1448 Fourth St.*

Shops at The Rink.

The Robinson House, designed by architect Henry Howard.

5 Commander's Palace.
Ordinarily, we'd recommend a snack stop here, but we're going to break our own rules. As long as you're in the Garden District you might as well make the most of your time. If you're going to eat at one New Orleans restaurant, it should be Commander's Palace, the crown jewel in the Brennan family dining dynasty. See p 103. *1403 Washington Ave.* ☎ *504/899-8221. $$$.*

6 Former site of Robb Mansion. If you're wondering what these suburban-styled brick ranches are doing in the middle of the tony Garden District, you're not the first to do so. Once an imposing private residence, then home to Newcomb College for Women, the mansion fell into disrepair and was demolished in 1954. The property was then subdivided for these modern houses. *1200 block of Washington Ave. (bordered by Chestnut, Camp & Sixth sts.).*

7 Musson-Bell House. Edgar Degas's French Creole uncle, Michel Musson, was one of the few non-Americans to live in this nouveau riche neighborhood. When he lost much of his wealth after the Civil

War, he moved to a slightly less ostentatious mansion on Esplanade Avenue among Creole society. (Degas visited him there and it is now known as the Degas House.) *1331 Third St.*

8 Robinson House. Architect Henry Howard created this extraordinary home for Walter Robinson, who moved from Virginia to New Orleans to become a cotton merchant, but instead went into his home state's best-known crop, tobacco. It took 6 years (1859–1865) to complete this massive home. Note the unusual curved portico; the roof was designed to collect rainwater and act as a cistern, thus pioneering indoor plumbing in the Garden District. *1415 Third St.*

9 Davis House. This gorgeous 1858 home belongs to the Women's Guild of the New Orleans Opera Association. It's one of the few area mansions available for special events. Opera was first performed in New Orleans in 1796 and has been staged nearly every year since. *2504 Prytania St.*

10 Our Lady of Perpetual Help Chapel. Originally built in 1858 as a private residence for wealthy

Payne-Strachan House.

merchant Henry Lonsdale, the home eventually served as a public chapel. Anne Rice attended Mass here as a girl and she caused quite a stir when she purchased the property as an adult. The vampire author never did quite fit in with her uptight, old-money neighbors (and she appeared to prefer it that way). Actor Nicolas Cage now owns the property, which has proven to be far less entertaining. *2521 Prytania St.*

⑪ Bradish Johnson House.
This stunning French Second-Empire home is now part of Louise S. McGehee School for Girls. Local architect James Freret studied in Paris and classical influence can be seen in many of his homes and buildings of the period. Sugar baron Bradish Johnson's ornate 1872 mansion cost $100,000—easily more than $1 million if someone built it today. *2343 Prytania St.*

⑫ Toby's Corner.
Despite owner Thomas Toby's attempt to build a cottage in the Northern tradition, the Greek Revival–styled cottage still borrows from the practical applications of local Creole architecture, such as being raised on brick piers for increased cooling. Dating back to 1838, this is the oldest house in the Garden District. *2340 Prytania St.*

⑬ Rosegate.
Anne Rice's former home was the first to be built on the block in 1856. It serves as the setting for her *Witching Hour* series. Look for the delicate rosette pattern in the fence, which gave the Greek Revival town house its name. When Rice resided here, Goth kids hung out on the street corner, waiting for her limo to show up so they could catch a glimpse of the famous vampire author. *1239 First St.*

⑭ Payne-Strachan House.
Built in 1849, this antebellum Greek Revival home is best known as the place where Jefferson Davis, president of the Confederacy, passed away in 1889 while visiting friends. *1134 First St.*

The raised brick piers underneath Toby's Corner allows for better cooling.

Uptown

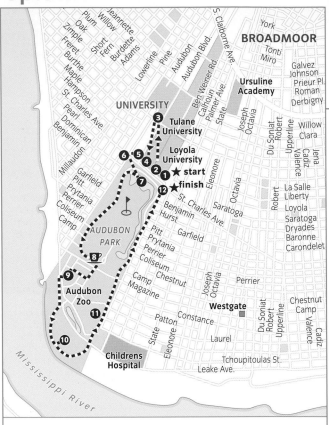

Area of detail

0   1/2 mi

0   0.5 km

1. Loyola University
2. Holy Name of Jesus Church
3. Tulane University
4. Gibson Hall
5. Zemurray Mansion
6. Parkview Guesthouse
7. Audubon Park
8. Audubon Park Clubhouse
9. Audubon Zoo
10. The Fly
11. Audubon Park Oak
12. Round Table Clubhouse

When I think of Uptown, I remember my first apartment in a two-story Victorian home and the freedom of being able to walk anywhere I needed to go. A little family grocery was around the block, Audubon Park was 10 minutes away on foot, and the St. Charles Streetcar was easy to catch. No matter where you wander, you'll see historic mansions, giant live oak trees, and friendly faces. Bounded by the Mississippi River and Carrollton, Claiborne, and Jackson avenues, this is the largest neighborhood in the city.

START: St. Charles Avenue between Loyola and Tulane universities.

Loyola University.

❶ Loyola University. Jesuits were early pioneers in shaping New Orleans' history, including introducing sugar cane to the region in the late 18th century. In 1849, they

Gibson Hall at Tulane University.

opened the College of the Immaculate Conception downtown. As the college grew, they purchased a "suburban" tract of land across from Audubon Park for $22,500 in 1886. Loyola College opened its doors in 1906 and was granted a university charter in 1912. Today, the school serves over 2,600 undergrads and nearly 2,000 graduate students. *6363 St. Charles Ave. ☎ 800/456-9652 or 504/865-3240. www.loyno.edu.*

❷ Holy Name of Jesus Church. In 1913, when the parish outgrew its little wooden chapel, construction began on this larger church thanks to a $150,000 donation. It was completed in 1918. The large altar is carved of Carrara marble, cost $12,000 and was donated that same year. You can see the tall bell tower even from the far reaches of Audubon Park. Although the church still has its original 1892 bell, it was replaced by electric keyboard chimes

The Greek-Revival-style columns of the Zemurray Mansion.

which, surprisingly, sound just as lovely. *6367 St. Charles Ave. ☎ 504/865-7430. www.hnjchurch.org.*

③ Tulane University. My alma mater was founded by seven doctors in 1834 as the Medical College of Louisiana. In 1884, thanks to a generous $1-million donation from Paul Tulane, it became Tulane University of Louisiana, a private, nonsectarian school. The main campus moved to the Uptown location in 1894. Today, it's the largest private

The grand oak trees in Audubon Park.

employer in New Orleans. *6823 St. Charles Ave. ☎ 504/865-5000. www.tulane.edu.*

④ Gibson Hall. This massive neo-Romanesque building was built in 1894, the first to be constructed on the Uptown Tulane campus. *6823 St. Charles Ave. ☎ 504/865-5000. www.tulane.edu.*

⑤ Zemurray Mansion. Cotton broker and lumberman William T. Jay commissioned this formidable Greek Revival mansion in 1908, then sold it to fruit and produce importer Samuel Zemurray in 1917. His widow bequeathed the mansion to Tulane University and it's served as the Tulane president's residence ever since. *7000 St. Charles Ave.*

⑥ Parkview Guesthouse. This popular bed-and-breakfast was built as a boarding house in the late 1800s and is listed on the National Register of Historic Places. *7004 St. Charles Ave. ☎ 888/533-0746 or 504/861-7564. www.parkview guesthouse.com.*

⑦ kids Audubon Park. Named for John James Audubon, who briefly lived in the New Orleans area, the 340-acre (136-hectare) park provides plenty of activities,

On the porch at the Audubon Park Clubhouse.

from bird watching to golf. See p 84. *6500 St. Charles Ave. (across from Tulane and Loyola universities, nestled btw. St. Charles Ave. & Magazine St.).* ☎ *504/581-4629.*

⑧ Audubon Park Clubhouse. Head for a porch table so you can enjoy the park view while eating a sandwich in this casual cafe. The food is nothing to write home about, but it's convenient. *6500 Magazine St.* ☎ *504/212-5285. $.*

⑨ kids Audubon Zoo. In addition to your usual lions, tigers, and bears, the subtropical weather supports exhibits of animals that normally live in warm climates, including the impressive 6- to 9-foot-long (1.8m–2.7m) Komodo dragons, averaging 200 pounds, from Indonesia. One of my favorite places is Monkey Hill, a man-made hill for New Orleans kids to contrast the rest of the flat city. ⏱ *2–3 hr.* See p. 86, ❸. *6500 Magazine St.*

⑩ kids The Fly. Follow the curved road to the right of the zoo and you'll come to this riverside park. Locals nicknamed it "The Fly" because the land is in the shape of a butterfly bordered by the Mississippi River. It's fun to watch passing ships, tugboats, and tankers. *Riverview Dr. off of Magazine St. btw. Audubon Zoo and the Mississippi River.*

⑪ Audubon Park Oak. After walking along the river, head back toward Magazine Street to see one of the largest live oaks. The trunk measures more than 35 feet (11m) around and the spread of the "crown" (overhead branches) is 165 feet (50m) across. *Btw. the Fly and Magazine St.*

⑫ Round Table Clubhouse. This charming historic home serves as headquarters to an exclusive men's social club organized in 1898. *6330 St. Charles Ave.*

Esplanade Ridge

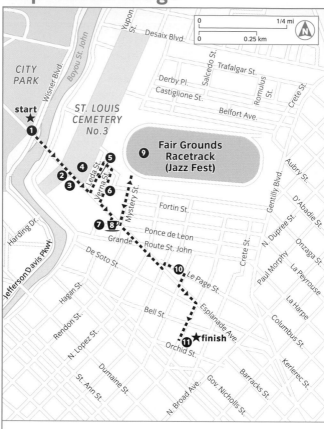

1. The General P.G.T. Beauregard
   Equestrian Statue
2. Cabrini High School
3. Old streetcar barn
4. St. Louis Cemetery No. 3
5. Luling Mansion
6. Verna Street bungalows
7. Terranova's
8. Fair Grinds Coffee House
9. Fair Grounds Race Course
10. Cresson House
11. Dufour-Plasson House

O n Esplanade Avenue, the sounds of city life are muffled by giant oak trees whose massive roots twist the sidewalks into roller coasters. To add to the exotic atmosphere, bright green monk parakeets call out with an unmistakable squawk. In the spring, confederate jasmine perfumes the entire neighborhood. In the summer, delicate crepe myrtle trees are in full bloom. Block after block of imposing historic homes—from Victorians to raised villas—remind us that this was the Creole upper class's answer to the American elite's Garden District. START: **Esplanade Avenue at Wisner Boulevard, between City Park and Bayou St. John. Cross the bridge over the bayou and continue on Esplanade.**

❶ The General P.G.T. Beauregard Equestrian Statue. This statue was completed in 1915 and is on the National Register of Historic Places. It's one of three monuments representing the "Cult of the Lost Cause," an outlook shared by many Southerners after the Civil War. General Pierre Gustave Toutant Beauregard was one of three Confederate soldiers elevated to hero status in order to glorify what loyalists saw as a noble struggle. (Statues of Robert E. Lee and Jefferson Davis are also located in the city.) He lived lavishly in the French Quarter in the Beauregard-Keyes House. *Traffic circle at Esplanade Ave. and Wisner Blvd., directly across from main entrance to City Park.*

The P.G.T. Beauregard equestrian statue.

Formerly an orphanage, Cabrini High School is now a Catholic high school for girls.

❷ Cabrini High School. Young girls whose parents succumbed to yellow fever found sanctuary in the orphanage with its founder, Saint Frances Xavier Cabrini. By 1959, there was no longer a need for the orphanage and the sisters opened Cabrini Catholic High School for girls. The campus extends back behind Esplanade to a two-story complex built around 1965 on Moss Street overlooking Bayou St. John. Personal and group tours of the shrine, chapel, and/or school are available to individuals, schools, and church groups by calling the Campus Minister at ☎ 504/483-8690. 🕐 *15–45 min. Back of campus on*

The Carrollton Streetcar barn.

Moss St. overlooking Bayou St. John; original school entrance, 3400 Esplanade Ave. ☎ 504/483-8690. Free admission. Tours by appointment only.

③ Old streetcar barn. This is one of the few surviving streetcar stations from the late 1800s for streetcars and the mules that pulled them. The New Orleans City Railroad Company began to convert to electricity in 1885 and gradually the mules were no longer needed. *Esplanade Ave. across from St. Louis Cemetery No. 3.*

④ St. Louis Cemetery No. 3. Home to wealthy Creole families in the mid- to late 1800s, the cemetery remains active and well cared for. You can safely walk around without a tour group. See p 22, ③. *3421 Esplanade Ave.*

⑤ Luling Mansion. Originally a private residence, it became the "Jockey Club" in 1871 for the new Fairgrounds racetrack. It once lorded over Esplanade Avenue, but smaller homes soon invaded in the 1920s. Look for the cursive "L" on the concrete fence posts. The building has been converted to apartments, although the owner lives on-site and has painstakingly renovated it to its former glory. *1436 Leda Court.*

⑥ Verna Street bungalows. The bungalow style was very popular in early- to mid-20th-century New Orleans and this street shows off a few in succession. At the corner of Marie and Verna streets, look for the gargoyle-cum-trumpet-player whose hair is on fire keeping watch over the entry to this cozy bungalow (*1459 Verna St.*). Further down the block, you'll find an eye-catching, bright purple bungalow with a rooftop deck (*1445 Verna St.*). Kitty-cornered across the street is a stunning two-story bungalow featuring a vibrant color palette of violet, sunset orange, and olive green with complementary landscaping (*1432 Verna St.*).

⑦ Terranova's. This place is a rarity these days: a small family-run grocery and convenience store. The third generation of Terranovas will help you find anything from a choice cut of meat to the best local hangouts. *3308 Esplanade Ave. ☎ 504/482-4131. Mon–Fri 8am–6:30pm, Sat 9am–6:30pm. Closed Sun.*

8 Fair Grinds Coffee House.
Painted tables and chairs, equally colorful locals, and strong iced coffee make for an eye-opening combination. Cash only. *3133 Ponce de Leon St. y 504/948-3222. $.*

9 Fair Grounds Race Course.
This is one of the oldest racetracks in the country, founded in 1872. The racing season runs from Thanksgiving Day to late March. It's also host to the famous New Orleans Jazz & Heritage Festival the last two weekends of April. See p. 41. *1751 Gentilly Blvd.*

10 Cresson House.
This grand and unique turreted Queen Anne was built in 1902. The lovely fleur-de-lis gate is a study in contrasts with the delicate design in heavy cast iron. You can go farther down Esplanade, but I strongly recommend that you do not cross Broad Street on foot. Please be careful

The bungalow at 1445 Verna St.

Inside Fair Grinds Coffee House.

and alert at all times. *2809 Esplanade Ave.*

11 Dufour-Plasson House.
This 1870 mansion is relatively young compared to the historic houses you'll see on the bayou. In 1906, it was moved from Esplanade to its current location. The whimsically painted cornstalk and sunflower cast-iron fence and old brick sidewalk add to its charms. *1206 North White St.*

Bayou St. John

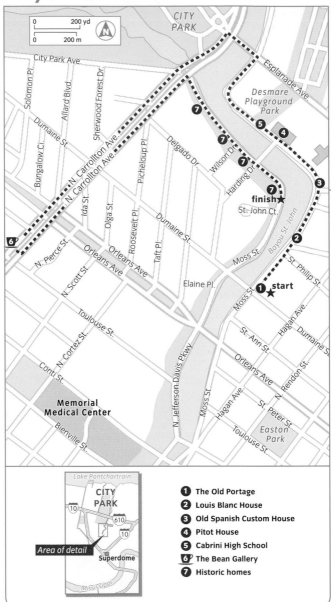

1 The Old Portage

2 Louis Blanc House

3 Old Spanish Custom House

4 Pitot House

5 Cabrini High School

6 The Bean Gallery

7 Historic homes

Once a busy waterway used by Native Americans, Bayou St. John now offers a sleepy respite from urban life. You may either follow the sidewalk for a close-up view of the cottages, shotgun houses (a house described as laid out in such a straight line that you could shoot a shotgun through the front door and the bullet would go straight out the back door), and Greek Revival homes or scramble down the small grassy levee to the edge of the water and look for fish, turtles, frogs, and ducks. When you cross Grand Route St. John, you're standing on the oldest street in New Orleans, originally a Native American portage between the bayou and the Mississippi River. In 1699, the Biloxi Indians guided French Louisiana colonists and brothers Pierre Le Moyne, Sieur d'Iberville, and Jean-Baptiste Le Moyne, Sieur de Bienville, through what is now Grand Route St. John. START: **Take the Canal Streetcar to Jefferson Davis Parkway stop, head north to beginning of bayou.**

❶ The Old Portage. From this historic landmark on the bayou side of the street you can spot birds, turtles, pelicans (on occasion), jumping fish, little diving birds, cranes, egrets, and ducks. Ellen Barkin was filmed jogging along the bayou for the 1987 movie *The Big Easy* costarring Dennis Quaid. 🕐 *10 min. On the bayou side of the intersection of Moss and Bell sts.*

❷ Louis Blanc House. One of the oldest homes on the bayou (predating the Louisiana Purchase of 1803) is located on shady Moss Street, named for the Spanish moss hanging from live oak trees bordering the bayou. 🕐 *10 min. 924 Moss St.*

❸ Old Spanish Custom House. Believed to be the oldest surviving residence in New Orleans, this elegant two-story, West Indies–style plantation home was built in 1784 and sold for just over $1 million at auction in 2009. Hundreds of people took advantage of the public open house in the days leading up to the auction, eager to satiate their curiosity about the nearly 3,000-square-foot (279-sq.-m) colonial mansion. It's unknown whether the winning bidder, Lyndon Saia,

Louis Blanc House.

who grew up in the neighborhood, will maintain it as a private residence or open it to the public. At one time, it overlooked flatboat traffic from Lake Pontchartrain to the French Quarter via the bayou to a man-made canal built in the 19th century by Spanish Governor Carondelet that was filled in more than 50

The wide galleries on the Pitot House are typical of West-Indies-style architecture.

years ago. The only boats you'll see these days are canoes and the occasional rowboat. 🕐 *10 min. 1300 Moss St. at Grand Route St. John.*

4 Pitot House. This house was built around 1799 for James Pitot, the first mayor of incorporated New Orleans. This is an excellent example of a West Indies–style plantation home, featuring wide galleries, large rounded columns, and a weathered wooden fence. In 1962, a proposed expansion of the neighboring high school threatened its existence. The Louisiana Landmarks Society moved the house a block away to save it from the wrecking ball. *1440 Moss St.*

5 Cabrini High School. The namesake of this Catholic high school for girls was an extraordinary woman, having founded the first missionary order of women, the Missionary Sisters of the Sacred Heart of Jesus. She also was named the first American Citizen Saint, Patroness of the Immigrants, and inducted into the National Women's Hall of Fame. See p 63, **2**.

Cross the bridge over the bayou. Cross Carrollton Avenue then head southwest a couple blocks to the intersection of Carrollton Avenue and St. Peter Street.

The Voodoo Queen of Bayou St. John

Voodoo in New Orleans is a unique combination of beliefs borrowed from African animism, Haitian spirits, and Roman Catholicism. The latter was likely incorporated to placate the local authorities. Even so, the city's European population feared voodoo and its practitioners. In fact, in the late 18th century, Spanish Governor Galvez wouldn't allow slaves from Martinique into the city because he believed that their devotion to voodoo made them dangerous. Police raids in the French Quarter became common enough that voodoo practitioners went out to the "country" along Bayou St. John. Priestess **Marie Laveau** (1801–1881), a free woman of color, was particularly influential. She made good use of her connections with servants throughout the city, and knew secrets about the elite that were attributed to black magic but were most likely due to spying, blackmail, and her early career as a hairstylist to the wealthy. Nevertheless, she drew thousands of believers to the "Wishing Spot" on the bayou. They supposedly drank the blood of roosters and danced with snakes, the earthly symbol of the voodoo god.

The Old Spanish Custom House may be the oldest surviving residence in New Orleans.

⑥ The Bean Gallery. The strong Turkish coffee will give you a much needed energy boost. Choose from fresh pastries and healthy sandwiches to fuel up for more walking. *637 N. Carrollton Ave.* ☎ *504/324-8176. $.*

An assortment of goodies on offer at the Bean Gallery.

Cross Carrollton Avenue again, head northeast for a block or two then turn right on West Moss Street so you can explore the southwest side of Bayou St. John.

⑦ Historic homes. Whether you choose to follow the sidewalk for a closer look or view them from across the street along the bayou, you'll see block after block of cottage, Colonial, Victorian, Greek Revival, and shotgun homes. The different styles serve as a veritable timeline of when they were built as the city's drainage system improved, allowing for more residential development, particularly by the wealthy in search of a country home. Feel free to turn right on Harding Drive which will intersect again with Moss Street after a few blocks. ⏱ *30 min. 800–1500 blocks of West Moss St.*

Carrollton

Harrell Stadium and Center

LEONIDAS

St. John Baptist Church

OAK STREET SHOPPING AREA

St. Andrew Episcopal Church

EAST CARROLLTON

RIVERBEND SHOPPING AREA

finish ★ 13

MAPLE STREET SHOPPING AREA

TULANE UNIVERSITY

UPTOWN CARROLLTON

★ start

Palmer Park

METAIRIE

FRENCH QUARTER

BRIDGE CITY

Superdome

MARRERO

Area of detail

1 Palmer Park
2 Nix-Arensman House
3 Carrollton Streetcar Barn
4 Weston Ward House
5 Sully-Wormuth-Langfels House
6 rue de la course
7 8100–8500 blocks Oak Street shopping
8 The Riverbend shopping
9 Wilkinson House
10 D'Antoni House
11 7500–8000 blocks Maple Street browsing
12 Lusher Charter School
13 Camellia Grill

Carrollton is nestled into a bend in the Mississippi River nearly 6 miles (9.7km) from the Quarter via the St. Charles Streetcar. Incorporated as the city of Carrollton in 1833, the city of New Orleans annexed it in 1874. The main thoroughfare is Carrollton Avenue, which is shaded by massive oaks like its more famous cousin, St. Charles Avenue. It's a very walkable neighborhood with plenty of coffeehouses and shopping on Oak and Maple streets and in the Riverbend. START: **End of the streetcar line at Carrollton and Claiborne avenues.**

1 Palmer Park. Among the large live oaks are a World War II memorial and a plaque commemorating the City of New Orleans annexing the Town of Carrollton in 1874. Local nonprofit Parkway Partners plans to renovate the park and build an 1,800-square-foot (167-sq.-m) tourist welcome center within the next few years. *Bounded by Carrollton and Claiborne aves., and Dublin and Sycamore sts.*

2 Nix-Arensman House. Though it appears much younger, this eclectic Arts and Crafts–style brick home was built nearly a century ago, in 1915. Both brick and stone are used for the battered columns, which is an unusual feature. *2130 S. Carrollton Ave., at Sycamore Place, southeast corner of Palmer Park.*

3 Carrollton Streetcar Barn. Peek inside to see the St. Charles line streetcars get repaired or prepped for their leisurely route. If you follow the tracks, you'll understand why no

Italianate detail on the Weston Ward House.

off-street parking is allowed for the residents of the streets bordering the barn. Be doubly careful when you cross the street! *Half-block off of Carrollton Ave., btw. Jeannette, Dublin, and Willow sts.*

The Arts and Crafts–style Nix-Arensman House.

④ Weston Ward House. This lemon-yellow Victorian home dates back to the late 19th century and features delicate Italianate details. *1537 S. Carrollton Ave.*

⑤ Sully-Wormuth-Langfels House. A stunning combination of Queen Anne and Colonial Revival elements, the locally renowned architect Thomas Sully designed and built this home in 1893 as his office and personal residence. *1531 S. Carrollton Ave.*

⑥ rue de la course. Step inside this converted early-19th-century bank building for European-style coffee and pastries. The sandwiches are okay; you're better off with a warm almond croissant. *1140 S. Carrollton Ave.* ☎ *504/861-4343. $.*

⑦ 8100–8500 blocks Oak Street shopping. After a rough couple of decades, this unique main street is flourishing once again, offering antiques, clothing, books, jewelry, cafes, bars, and more. *Btw. Carrollton Ave. and Leonidas St.*

⑧ The Riverbend shopping. Independent boutique shops like Yvonne La Fleur (*8131 Hampson St.* ☎ *504/866-9666*) and familiar commercial chain stores now occupy the former site of a 19th-century public open market. Go behind the mini strip mall to find a tiny park and modest Victorian-homes-turned-restaurants and shops. *Bounded by Carrollton and Leake aves. and Maple St.*

⑨ Wilkinson House. This striking and rare Tudor Gothic home was built by Englishman Nathaniel Wilkinson in 1849. The mansion and its manicured lawn and gardens cover half a city block. *1015 S. Carrollton Ave.*

⑩ D'Antoni House. If you like the Prairie style, you'll love this massive brick villa designed by Edward Sport and built in 1917. Note the complementary garage and intricately detailed iron fence surrounding the sprawling property. *7929 Freret St.*

⑪ 7500–8000 Maple Street browsing. Around here you'll find a mix of cute Victorian shotgun homes and cottages among restaurants and small businesses, including local hangouts PJ's Coffee & Tea (*7624 Maple St.* ☎ *504/866-7031*) and Maple Street Book Shop (*7529 Maple St.* ☎ *504/861-2105*).

⑫ Lusher Charter School. Designed by architect Henry Howard, the Lusher Charter School was originally built in 1854 to serve as Carrollton's courthouse and town hall. The massive neoclassical columns now support one of the finest, most diverse public charter schools in the city. *719 S. Carrollton Ave.*

⑬ Camellia Grill. Ask for a slice of fried pecan pie and wash it down with a thick vanilla shake. *626 S. Carrollton Ave.* ☎ *504/866-9573. $.* ●

Camellia Grill is known for their delicious pecan pie.

Shopping Best Bets

Best **T-Shirt Designs**
Metro Three, *2032 Magazine St.*
(p 79)

Best **Shoe Store**
★★ Feet First, *4119 Magazine St.
and 526 Royal St. (p 76 and p 79)*

Best **Art Supplies Store**
National Art & Hobby, *5835 Magazine St. (p 78)*

Best **Contemporary Home
Furnishings**
★★★ Cameron Jones, *2127 Maga-
zine St. (p 81)*

Best **Wood Furniture**
Wilkerson Row, *3137 Magazine St.
(p 81)*

Best **Fine Lingerie**
★★ House of Lounge, *2044 Magazine St. (p 79)*

Biggest **Collection of Cajun &
Jazz Music**
★★★ Louisiana Music Factory,
210 Decatur St. (p 82)

Best **Gallery**
★ A Gallery for Fine Photography,
241 Chartres St. (p 80)

Best **Department Store**
Saks Fifth Avenue, *301 Canal St.
(p 80)*

Best **Glassware**
Hugh Martin Home, *4222A Magazine St. (p 81)*

Best **Hip & Wearable
Women's Fashion**
Trashy Diva, *829 Chartres St. and
2048 Magazine St. (p 76 and p 79)*

Best **Place for Makeover**
★★ Fifi Mahony's, *934 Royal St.
(p 79)*

Best **Vintage Clothing**
Le Garage, *1234 Decatur St. (p 79)*

Best **Place for Antiques**
Keil's Antiques, *325 Royal St.
(p 77)*

Best **Wine Store**
Martin Wine Cellar, *3500 Magazine
St. (p 80)*

Best **Chocolates**
★ Blue Frog Chocolates, *5707
Magazine St. (p 80)*

Best **Pralines**
Southern Candymakers, *334 Decatur St. (p 80)*

Best **Museum Shop**
★★ National World War II
Museum, *945 Magazine St. (p 81)*

Best **Secondhand Book Shop**
George Herget Used Books, *3109
Magazine St. (p 78)*

Best **Modern Book Shop**
★★★ Octavia Books, *513 Octavia
St. (p 78)*

Best **Tunes**
★★ The Mushroom, *1037 Broadway. (p 82)*

Previous page: An impressive display of toys on sale at the Idea Factory.

Royal Street Shopping

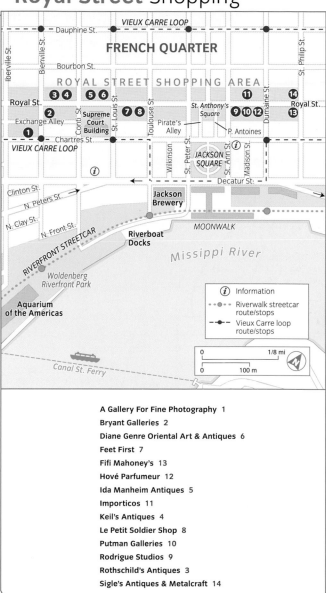

A Gallery For Fine Photography 1

Bryant Galleries 2

Diane Genre Oriental Art & Antiques 6

Feet First 7

Fifi Mahoney's 13

Hové Parfumeur 12

Ida Manheim Antiques 5

Importicos 11

Keil's Antiques 4

Le Petit Soldier Shop 8

Putman Galleries 10

Rodrigue Studios 9

Rothschild's Antiques 3

Sigle's Antiques & Metalcraft 14

Magazine Street Shopping

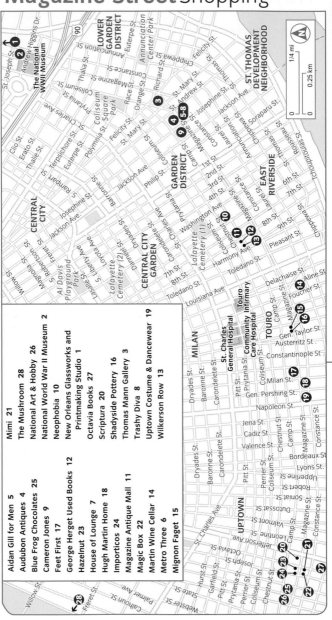

Aidan Gill for Men **5**
Audubon Antiques **4**
Blue Frog Chocolates **25**
Cameron Jones **9**
Feet First **17**
George Herget Used Books **12**
Hazelnut **23**
House of Lounge **7**
Hugh Martin Home **18**
Importicos **24**
Magazine Antique Mall **11**
Magic Box **22**
Martin Wine Cellar **14**
Metro Three **6**
Mignon Faget **15**

Mimi **21**
The Mushroom **28**
National Art & Hobby **26**
National World War II Museum **2**
Neophobia **10**
New Orleans Glassworks and
    Printmaking Studio **1**
Octavia Books **27**
Scriptura **20**
Shadyside Pottery **16**
Thomas Mann Gallery **3**
Trashy Diva **8**
Uptown Costume & Dancewear **19**
Wilkerson Row **13**

French Quarter Shopping

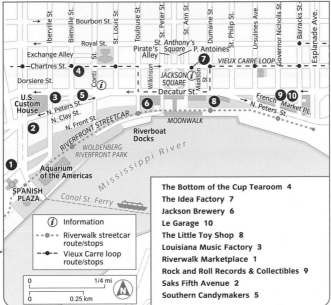

The Bottom of the Cup Tearoom 4
The Idea Factory 7
Jackson Brewery 6
Le Garage 10
The Little Toy Shop 8
Louisiana Music Factory 3
Riverwalk Marketplace 1
Rock and Roll Records & Collectibles 9
Saks Fifth Avenue 2
Southern Candymakers 5

Shopping A to Z

Antiques

Audubon Antiques MAGAZINE STREET This two-story treasure stocks everything from curios to authentic antiques. *2025 Magazine St.* ☎ *504/581-5704. AE, MC, V. Map p 76.*

Diane Genre Oriental Art and Antiques ROYAL STREET If you need a break from heavy European antiques, be refreshed by East Asian porcelains, 18th-century Japanese woodblock prints, and Chinese and Japanese textiles. By appointment only; call ahead. *431 Royal St.* ☎ *504/595-8945. www.dianegenre orientalart.com. MC, V. Map p 75.*

Ida Manheim Antiques ROYAL STREET Proprietor Ida Manheim's grandfather started the business in 1919 in this same location and she continues the family tradition of Continental, English, and Oriental furnishings, along with porcelain, jade, silver, and fine paintings. *403–409 Royal St.* ☎ *504/568-1901 or 888/627-5969. www.idamanheimantiques.com. AE, DISC, MC, V. Map p 75.*

Keil's Antiques ROYAL STREET Established in 1899 and run by Peter Moss, great-grandson of the founder, Keil's has a considerable collection of 18th- and 19th-century French and English furniture, chandeliers, and jewelry. *325 Royal St.*

Ida Manheim Antiques.

☎ *504/522-4552. www.keilsantiques. com. AE, MC, V. Map p 75.*

Magazine Antique Mall MAGA-ZINE STREET   Twenty-eight independent dealers show off their wares, including 18th- and 19th-century furnishings, music boxes, dollhouse miniatures, porcelain, and antique toys. *3017 Magazine St.* ☎ *504/895-5451. AE, MC, V. Map p 76.*

Rothschild's Antiques ROYAL STREET   This fourth-generation-run antiques store and full-service jeweler will have you fantasizing about a home makeover in no time. *321 Royal St.* ☎ *504/523-5816 or 523-2281. MC, V. Map p 75.*

Sigle's Antiques & Metalcraft ROYAL STREET   Sigle's specializes in delicate ironwork, like that you've seen in the French Quarter. Stop in here and take home a unique souvenir. *935 Royal St.* ☎ *504/522-7647. MC, V. Map p 75.*

Art Supplies
National Art & Hobby MAGA-ZINE STREET   Get creative with everything from crafts to paintbrushes to scrapbooking supplies. *5835 Magazine St.* ☎ *504/899-4491. MC, V. Map p 76.*

Beauty Products & Cosmetics
Aidan Gill for Men MAGAZINE STREET   In addition to luxury soaps and handmade shaving accessories, Irish proprietor Aidan Gill and staff offer hairstyling and "The Shave at the End of the Galaxy," an old-fashioned hot-towel shave. *2026 Magazine St.* ☎ *504/587-9090. www. aidangillformen.com. AE, MC, V. Map p 76.*

Hové Parfumeur ROYAL STREET For more than 75 years, the family-run Hové has created original perfumes, colognes, body oils, lotions, and soaps, and currently offers 53 original fragrances, including the popular Tea Olive, Vetivert, and Creole Days. *824 Royal St.* ☎ *504/525-7827. www.hoveparfumeur.com. AE, DISC, MC, V. Map 75.*

Books & Stationery
George Herget Used Books MAGAZINE STREET   Browse thousands of rare and used books in a cozy atmosphere. *3109 Magazine St.* ☎ *504/891-5595. No credit cards. Map p 76.*

★★★ **Octavia Books** UPTOWN Husband-and-wife proprietors Tom Lowenburg and Judith Lafitte renovated this 100-year-old former grocery into a modern yet inviting bookstore where you can wander among the stacks or lounge on the outdoor patio and listen to the waterfall cascade into a small goldfish-stocked pond. *513 Octavia St.* ☎ *504/899-READ [7323]. www.octaviabooks.com. MC, V. Map p 76.*

Scriptura MAGAZINE STREET Wordsmiths will love this full-service, upscale stationer, which sells custom invitations, engraved and embossed stationery, leather journals, address books, desk accessories, wine journals, photo albums, and fine writing instruments. *5423 Magazine St.* ☎ *504/897-5555. www.scriptura.com. AE, MC, V. Map p 76.*

Clothing & Shoes
★★ **Feet First** ROYAL STREET/MAGAZINE STREET Shoes, handbags, and accessories galore, with new inventory added every week. The crowded shelves feature more than 50 designers—from Michael Kors to Kate Spade—plus local favorites Dirty Coast, NOLA Couture, and Feelgoodz. *4119 Magazine St.* ☎ *504/899-6800, and 526 Royal St.* ☎ *504/569-0005. www.feetfirststores.com. AE, DISC, MC, V. Map p 76.*

★★ **Fifi Mahony's** ROYAL STREET Don't wait for Mardi Gras season to splurge on a funky wig, hair accessories, and makeup necessities by Ben Nye, Urban Decay, Tony and Tina, Cookie Puss, or Fifi's own line. *934 Royal St.* ☎ *504/525-4343. www.fifi-mahoney.com. MC, V. Map p 75.*

★★ **House of Lounge** MAGAZINE STREET All you need to know is that the real Erin Brockovich spent lots of money here on designer lingerie and loungewear. *2044 Magazine St.* ☎ *504/671-8300. www.houseoflounge.com. MC, V. Map p 76.*

Le Garage DECATUR STREET On offer is an ever-changing selection of retro and vintage clothing. *1234 Decatur St.* ☎ *504/522-6639. MC, V. Map p 77.*

Metro Three MAGAZINE STREET If your friends are only going to get a T-shirt as a souvenir, then skip the raunchy offerings on Bourbon Street in favor of these creative and clever alternatives. *2032 Magazine St.* ☎ *504/558-0212. www.metrothree.com. MC, V. Map p 76.*

Mimi MAGAZINE STREET Model the latest fashions and accessories from this upscale boutique. *5500 Magazine St.* ☎ *504/269-6464. www.miminola.com. AE, MC, V. Map p 76.*

Trashy Diva MAGAZINE STREET Designer-owner Candice Gwinn brings back old-world glamour with her ultra-feminine dresses, blouses, jackets, and lingerie. *829 Chartres St.* ☎ *504/581-4555, and 2048 Magazine St.* ☎ *504/299-8777. www.trashydiva.com. AE, MC, V. Map p 75 and p 76.*

Uptown Costume & Dancewear MAGAZINE STREET If you like to play dress up, this is the place for you; lots of hats, wigs, makeup, and masks to help your transformation. *4326 Magazine St.* ☎ *504/895-7969. AE, MC, V. Map p 76.*

Hové Parfumeur has a scent for just about everyone.

Department Store
Saks Fifth Avenue FRENCH QUARTER   The upscale store offers designer clothing, shoe and handbag collections galore, plus jewelry, housewares, fine beauty products, and more. *The Shops at Canal Place, 301 Canal St. ☎ 504/524-2200. www.saksfifthavenue.com. AE, DISC, MC, V. Map p 77.*

Food, Chocolates & Wine
★ **Blue Frog Chocolates** MAGAZINE STREET   It's impossible to resist Fancy's "Sin in a Tin" toffees or delectable French truffles, so go ahead, indulge. *5707 Magazine St. ☎ 504/269-5707. www.bluefrog chocolates.com. MC, V. Map p 76.*

Martin Wine Cellar MAGAZINE STREET   Browse an impressive array of wines, spirits, and champagnes, plus preserves, coffee, tea, crackers, cookies, and cheese. *3500 Magazine St. ☎ 504/894-7420. www.martinwinecellar.com. AE, DISC, MC, V. Map p 76.*

Southern Candymakers DECATUR STREET   Satisfy your sweet tooth with Mississippi Mud squares, alligator- and crawfish-shaped chocolates, caramel turtles, sugar-coated pecans, hand-dipped ice cream, among other delights. *334 Decatur St. ☎ 504/523-5544 or 800/344-9773. www.southern candymakers.com. AE, MC, V. Map p 77.*

Galleries
Bryant Galleries ROYAL STREET A variety of contemporary mediums including glasswork, sculpture, and graphic art mingle with classic paintings and vintage photography by American and European artists. *316 Royal St. ☎ 800/844-1994 or 504/525-5584. www.bryantgalleries.com. AE, MC, V. Map p 75.*

Contemporary design at Cameron Jones.

★ **A Gallery for Fine Photography** FRENCH QUARTER   Even if you can't afford an original 19th-century print, it's worth stepping inside to view the extensive photo collections with a focus on Southern artists and subjects. *241 Chartres St. ☎ 504/568-1313. www.agallery. com. AE, MC, V. Map p 75.*

kids Le Petit Soldier Shop ROYAL STREET   Locally designed and molded miniature soldiers recreate ancient and modern battles, plus medals and decorations. *528 Royal St. ☎ 504/523-7741. MC, V. Map p 75.*

New Orleans Glassworks and Printmaking Studio MAGAZINE STREET   With New Orleans' infamous heat and humidity, this is the last place where you'd expect a glassworks studio, complete with 800-pound furnace. Their demonstrations are very cool. *727 Magazine St. ☎ 504/529-7277. www. neworleansartworks.com. AE, MC, V. Map p 76.*

Putman Galleries ROYAL STREET Collectors of African-American and Southern art will enjoy perusing the region's largest selection of posters and prints. *730 Royal St. ☎ 800/621-6179 or 504/523-7882. www. putmangallery.com. MC, V. Map p 75.*

Rodrigue Studios ROYAL STREET   What does it say about

art appreciation that artist George Rodrigue toiled in obscurity painting dark, moody, and critically acclaimed Cajun landscapes, but found fame and fortune when he started painting his beloved late dog in bright blue? If you're not familiar with the critically panned but publicly embraced Blue Dog icon, do come in. *721 Royal St.* ☎ *504/581-4244. www.george rodrigue.com. AE, MC, V. Map p 75.*

Gift Shops
The Bottom of the Cup Tea-room CHARTRES STREET   Opened in 1927 and supposedly the oldest tearoom in the United States, here you can browse holistic books, jewelry, tarot cards, crystals, and healing wands. *327 Chartres St.* ☎ *504/524-1997. www.bottomofthecup.com. MC, V. Map p 77.*

★★ National World War II Museum MAGAZINE STREET Features World War II–themed books, clothing, model airplanes, watches, and more. *945 Magazine St.* ☎ *504/527-6012. www.dday museum.org. MC, V. Map p 76.*

Housewares, Furnishings & Art
★★★ Cameron Jones MAGAZINE STREET   Playfully contemporary

George Rodrigue is most famous for his "Blue Dog" paintings.

furniture, lamps, and other home accessories are what make this shop a fun stop. *2127 Magazine St.* ☎ *504/524-3119. AE, MC, V. Map p 76.*

Hazelnut MAGAZINE STREET   Stop in for elegant home furnishings, including decorative accessories, and glassware, plus unusual New Orleans–themed gifts. *5515 Magazine St.* ☎ *504/891-2424. www. hazelnutneworleans.com. MC, V. Map p 76.*

Hugh Martin Home MAGAZINE STREET   Stocking the space are contemporary furniture, lamps, glassware, and gifts. *4222A Magazine St.* y *504/899-1882. MC, V. Map p 76.*

Importicos ROYAL STREET/MAGAZINE STREET   This place reminds me of a funkier World Market featuring colorful furniture, figurines, and more by international and local artists. *736 Royal St.* ☎ *504/523-3100, and 5523 Magazine St.* ☎ *504/891-6141. MC, V. Map p 76.*

Neophobia MAGAZINE STREET Vintage furniture, clothes, and collectibles from the 1950s, 1960s, and 1970s. *2855 Magazine St.* ☎ *504/899-2444. www.neophobia-nola. com. MC, V. Map p 76.*

Wilkerson Row MAGAZINE STREET   Artist-owner Shaun Wilkerson's award-winning custom furniture designs are influenced by 19th-century New Orleans architecture. *3137 Magazine St.* ☎ *504/899-3311. www.wilkersonrow.com. MC, V. Map p 76.*

Jewelry
Mignon Faget MAGAZINE STREET   Local artist Mignon Faget creates fine jewelry inspired by nature and Louisiana icons. *3801 Magazine St.* ☎ *504/891-2005 or 800/375-7557. www.mignonfaget. com. MC, V. Map p 76.*

Thomas Mann Gallery MAGAZINE STREET

Artist-proprietor Thomas Mann designs "techno-romantic" jewelry (you'll know it when you see it) and carries contemporary furniture. *1804 Magazine St.* ☎ *504/581-2113. www.thomasmann.com. MC, V. Map p 76.*

The sign outside Louisiana Music Factory.

Music

★★★ Louisiana Music Factory DECATUR STREET   Overwhelmed by the wealth of regional music on display? Just ask a knowledgeable staff member (this ain't Best Buy!) to help you select the best Cajun, zydeco, R&B, jazz, blues, and gospel. *210 Decatur St.* ☎ *504/586-1094. www.louisianamusicfactory.com. AE, MC, V. Map p 77.*

★★ The Mushroom. UPTOWN There's a reason why this popular local indie boasts, "It's worth the trip!" You won't find a better selection of used CDs, LPs, DVDs, and live recordings. *1037 Broadway.* ☎ *504/866-6065. www.mushroomnola.com. AE, DISC, MC, V. Map p 76.*

Rock and Roll Records & Collectibles DECATUR STREET   You can easily pass an hour or two going through the comprehensive vinyl collection that goes beyond rock and roll. *1214 Decatur St.* ☎ *504/561-5683. MC, V. Map p 77.*

Shopping Centers

Jackson Brewery FRENCH QUARTER   The old "Jax" Brewery is now a complex of shops with a variety of offerings such as Cajun and Creole food, clothing, and souvenirs. *600 Decatur St.* ☎ *504/566-7245. www.jacksonbrewery.com. AE, MC, V. Map p 77.*

Riverwalk Marketplace FRENCH QUARTER   A covered mall running along the river from Poydras Street to the Convention Center, this is a popular venue that's surprisingly scenic. *1 Poydras St.* ☎ *504/522-1555. www.riverwalkmarketplace.com. AE, MC, V. Map p 77.*

Toys

The Idea Factory CHARTRES STREET   There's no cheapy plastic stuff here at this shop that offers old-fashioned wooden toys like alphabet and number blocks, trains, and pull toys. *838 Chartres St.* ☎ *504/524-5195. http://ideafactoryneworleans.com. MC, V. Map p 77.*

The Little Toy Shop DECATUR STREET   An extra special kid's shop, offering a spectrum of goods from unique dolls to wooden toys to miniature cars and trucks. *900 Decatur St.* ☎ *504/522-6588. AE, MC, V. Map p 77.*

Magic Box MAGAZINE STREET This specialty toy store featuring the latest and greatest or nostalgic favorites has something for kids of all ages. *5508 Magazine St.* ☎ *504/899-0117. www.magicboxneworleans.com. AE, MC, V. Map p 76.* ●

Audubon Park

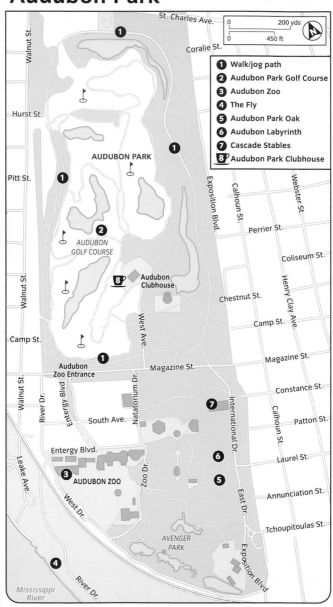

1 Walk/jog path
2 Audubon Park Golf Course
3 Audubon Zoo
4 The Fly
5 Audubon Park Oak
6 Audubon Labyrinth
7 Cascade Stables
8 Audubon Park Clubhouse

Previous page: Audubon Park.

Audubon Zoo

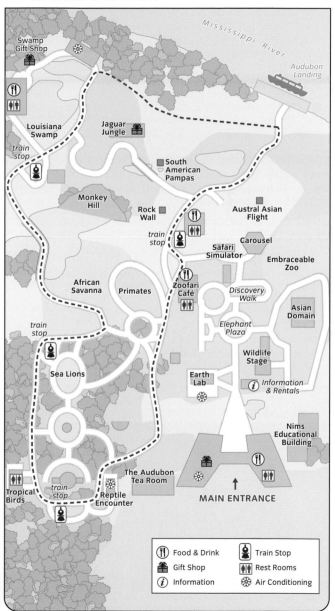

Mississippi River

Audubon Landing

Swamp Gift Shop

Louisiana Swamp

train stop

Jaguar Jungle

South American Pampas

Monkey Hill

Rock Wall

Austral Asian Flight

train stop

Carousel

Safari Simulator

Embraceable Zoo

African Savanna

Primates

Zoofari Café

Discovery Walk

Asian Domain

train stop

Elephant Plaza

Sea Lions

Wildlife Stage

Earth Lab

Information & Rentals

Nims Educational Building

Tropical Birds

train stop

Reptile Encounter

The Audubon Tea Room

MAIN ENTRANCE

🍴 Food & Drink	👤 Train Stop
🎁 Gift Shop	🚻 Rest Rooms
ⓘ Information	❄ Air Conditioning

As a college student and Uptown resident, I often sought quiet refuge in Audubon Park. The 340-acre (136-hectare) public park (which is privately owned by the Audubon Institute) was named after famed French-American naturalist and painter John James Audubon. (His mother was a French/Spanish Creole from Louisiana and he created much of his art in the pelican state.) This parcel of land was originally set aside to be a park in 1879, hosted the World's Fair in 1884, and officially opened as Audubon Park in 1886 with master-plan renovations by renowned park designer Frederick Law Olmsted in 1897. One of the World's Fair buildings, the 30-acre (12-hectare) Horticulture Hall, remained in use until a hurricane destroyed it in 1915. On the southern end of the park, live oaks, lagoons, gardens, and fountains offer a peaceful refuge amid the usual urban hustle and bustle. As you go north, you'll discover recreational opportunities such as golf, swimming, tennis, and the acclaimed Audubon Zoo. START: **6500 St. Charles Ave. (across from Tulane and Loyola universities, nestled btw. St. Charles Ave. and Magazine St.).**

❶ **Walk/jog paths.** Follow the nearly 2-mile (3.2km) asphalt track shaded by centuries-old live oak trees dripping with Spanish moss and enjoy colorful year-round landscaping and dreamy lagoons filled with birds, turtles, and fish. ⏱ *1 hr. Open daily sunrise–sunset.*

❷ **Audubon Park Golf Course.** *Golf Digest Magazine* named it the highest-rated golf course over a hundred years old in the country (though one has to

wonder how many century-old golf courses there are in the U.S.). Reserve your tee time by phone, at the Pro Shop, or online. ⏱ *2–4 hr. 6500 Magazine St. (btw. Walnut & Calhoun sts.).* ☎ *504/212-5290. www.auduboninstitute.org. Open Mon 11am–sunset, Tues–Sun 7am–sunset.*

❸ kids **Audubon Zoo.** I recommend you go early or late if you want to see the animals active in the outdoor exhibits, otherwise the hot

Walkers enjoy a quiet stroll in Audubon Park.

The entrance to the Audubon Zoo.

sun keeps them denned up and out of sight. Plan to eat before or after your visit as the food is expensive and just okay. ⏱ *2–3 hr. 6500 Magazine St.* ☎ *800/774-7394 or 504/581-4629. www.auduboninstitute. org. Admission $13 adults, $10 seniors, $8 children 2–12. Tues–Sun 10am–5pm.*

4 The Fly. This small Riverside Park is popular with locals for picnics, ball games, and watching boat and barge traffic down the Mississippi. *River Road off of Magazine St., along the Mississippi River.*

5 kids Audubon Park Oak. Measuring more than 35 feet (11m) around and 165 feet (50m) across its crown, you'd be hard pressed to manage a group hug touching hands. ⏱ *15 min. Btw. the Fly and Magazine St.*

6 kids Audubon Labyrinth. Unlike a maze where there are "dead ends," a labyrinth offers many different paths, none of which are wrong. Simply follow the stone path's twists and turns until you arrive at the center then return to the outer circle. ⏱ *20 min. East Dr. at Laurel St.* ☎ *504/304-4427. www.labyrinthat audubonpark.org. Free admission. Open daily sunrise–sunset.*

7 kids Cascade Stables. Your guide will take you on a 45-minute leisure ride around the perimeter of the park. The horses are always friendly and eager to go for a ride; children ages 7 and up are welcome to saddle up. ⏱ *1 hr.* ☎ *504/891-2246. www.cascadestables.net. $20 per ride. Reservations preferred. Tues–Sun 9am–4pm.*

8 Audubon Park Clubhouse. A convenient stop for sandwiches and a gorgeous park view. *6500 Magazine St.* ☎ *504/212-5285. $.*

A gorilla at the Audubon Zoo.

City Park

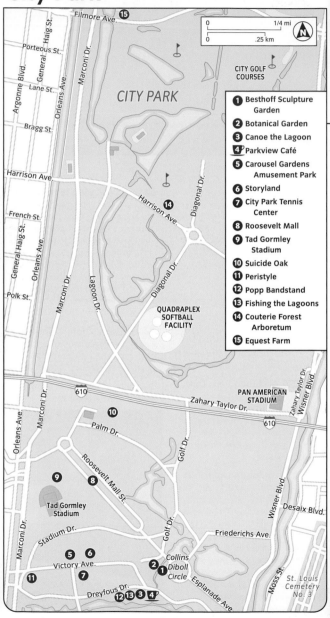

1/4 mi
.25 km

CITY GOLF COURSES

CITY PARK

QUADRAPLEX SOFTBALL FACILITY

PAN AMERICAN STADIUM

Tad Gormley Stadium

Collins Diboll Circle

St. Louis Cemetery No. 3

1 Besthoff Sculpture Garden
2 Botanical Garden
3 Canoe the Lagoon
4 Parkview Café
5 Carousel Gardens Amusement Park
6 Storyland
7 City Park Tennis Center
8 Roosevelt Mall
9 Tad Gormley Stadium
10 Suicide Oak
11 Peristyle
12 Popp Bandstand
13 Fishing the Lagoons
14 Couterie Forest Arboretum
15 Equest Farm

At 1,300 acres (520 hectares), City Park is the fifth largest urban park in the United States. The 150-year-old city oasis lost many of its mature live oaks—some more than 400 years old—to Hurricane Katrina devastation. Once the floodwaters receded, all of the grass, flowers, and bushes had died, coated in brown muck. A grass-roots effort by local citizens helped the park reblossom and again offer golf, tennis, horseback riding, walking trails, and kids' activities all surrounded by the natural beauty of giant oaks, lagoons, and wildlife. START: 1 Palm Dr., bounded by City Park Avenue and Canal, Lee, and Wisner boulevards.

① kids **Besthoff Sculpture Garden.** The 5-acre (2-hectare) garden contrasts a natural backdrop of mature, moss-draped oak trees with the clean lines of contemporary sculpture. My favorite pieces are Rona Pondick's haunting stainless steel *Monkeys,* George Segal's *Four Lines Oblique,* for its simplicity and graceful motion, and Jean-Michel Othoniel's whimsical *Tree of Necklaces.* The Besthoffs commissioned the latter, which are giant glass bead necklaces suspended from live oak branches, evoking the plastic beads caught in trees lining a Mardi Gras parade route. Kids will love Louise Bourgeois's giant bronze spider, but please, no climbing! ⏱ *1 hr. 1 Dueling Oaks Dr., adjacent to the New Orleans Museum of Art.* ☎ *504/658-4100. www.noma.org. Free admission. Wed–Sun 10am–4:45pm.*

Figures in the City Park Sculpture Garden.

② **The Botanical Gardens.** Hurricane Katrina flooding wiped out the garden's entire collection of orchids, staghorn ferns, bromeliads, and many more carefully cultivated plant species and old-growth trees. This was a devastating blow to one of the few remaining public gardens designed during the Works Progress Administration and Art Deco period of the 1930s. Thanks to dedicated staff and volunteers, the 12 acres (4.8 hectares) of Depression-era gardens, fountains, ponds, and sculptures, plus a horticultural library, are again open and thriving. The Historic Train Garden is an extraordinary and unique model of the City of New Orleans. As you follow the walkway, you'll see tiny streetcars and trains just like the ones that dutifully traveled the city from the late 1800s to the early 1900s. Each structure, made entirely out of botanical materials, has a real-life counterpart, including representative home styles organized by neighborhood. ⏱ *1 hr.* ☎ *504/483-9386. www.neworleanscitypark. com. Admission $6 adults, $3 children 5–12, free 4 and under. Tues–Sun 10am–4:30pm.*

③ kids **Canoe the Lagoon.** Take a relaxing ride in a pedal boat or canoe and explore up to 8 miles (13km) of lagoons. You'll see swans, ducks, geese, turtles, frogs, and fish. ⏱ *1 hr. Timken Center (old Casino Building), Dreyfous Dr.*

☎ 504/483-9371. Boat rental $5/per person per hour. Mar–Oct Sat–Sun 11am–3pm.

4 Parkview Café. This family-friendly place is perfect for resting your feet and snacking on sandwiches, salads, and desserts. If you absolutely must check your e-mail, there's free Wi-Fi, too. *Timken Center (old Casino Building), Dreyfous Dr.* ☎ *504/483-9371. $.*

5 kids Carousel Gardens Amusement Park. Kids of all ages love to ride the "flying horses" on the rare antique wooden carousel. It was built in 1910 and is one of only 100 antique carousels left in the country. It and the 1906 pavilion are on the National Register of Historic Places. Other cool rides include bumper cars, Red Baron miniplane, Tilt-A-Whirl, 40-foot (12m) fun slide, Ferris wheel, and more. A miniature train takes riders on a 2½-mile (4km) trip through the park. ⏱ *45 min. Dreyfous Dr.*

Kids make friends with a Storyland dragon.

☎ 504/482-4888. www.neworleans citypark.com. Admission $3 ages 3 and up, free 2 and under, rides $2–$4, unlimited ride band $15. Mar–Oct Sat–Sun 11am–6pm.

6 kids Storyland. More than 25 storybook-themed play areas feature colorful characters hand-sculpted by Mardi Gras float artists. Kids can climb in and out of Captain Hook's pirate ship, do a jig with the Three Little Pigs, explore the mouth of a whale with Pinocchio, or race up Jack & Jill's Hill. ⏱ *1 hr. Dreyfous Dr., next to Carousel Gardens.* ☎ *504/483-9381. Admission $3, free 2 and under. Tues–Fri 10am–3pm, Sat–Sun 11am–6pm.*

7 City Park Tennis Center. One of the largest public tennis facilities in the South has played host to numerous tournaments over the years. *Wisner Tennis Center, near corner of Victory and Anseman aves., across from Storyland.* ☎ *504/483-9383. www.neworleans citypark.com. Hard courts $7 per hr., Rubico clay courts $10 per hr. Mon–Thurs 8am–9pm, Fri–Sun 8am–6pm.*

8 Roosevelt Mall. This shady, half-mile (.8km) stretch of road and walkways is popular with joggers, dog walkers, and in-line skaters because it's one of the few New Orleans streets without significant bumps and potholes. You'll pass by kids playing softball in grassy fields and area high school track and field teams sweating it out on the track. In 1937, President Roosevelt personally dedicated the mall and other WPA projects in the park, including nearby Tad Gormley Stadium. ⏱ *30 min. From Lelong Ave. to Marconi Dr.*

9 Tad Gormley Stadium. Built as part of the WPA efforts, the stadium has played host to a number of icons, including Roosevelt, Dorothy Lamour selling war bonds in 1942, entertainers Bob Hope in

1944 and Roy Rogers and Trigger in 1959, and the legendary Beatles, who performed here in 1964. The stadium was remodeled in 1992 in preparation for the U.S. Olympic Track & Field trials that same year. 🕐 *10 min. Off of Roosevelt Mall and Marconi Dr.*

🔟 **Suicide Oak.** Measuring more than 22 feet (6.6m) in circumference and 65 feet (20m) high with a 124-foot (37m) crown, the Suicide Oak is one of the oldest and largest live oaks in the park. In the late 1800s and early 1900s many despondent people chose to end their lives here (thus the name), usually by hanging or self-inflicted gunshot wound. The last reported suicide took place in 1908. After the Huey P. Long Bridge was built in 1935, it replaced the Suicide Oak's sordid purpose. Sadly, the tree has seen better centuries. It required repair twice in the 1980s when it lost a pair of humongous limbs. One of them remains on the ground and is estimated to be more than 150 years old. 🕐 *10 min. Corner of Marconi Dr. and Victory Ave.*

⓫ **Peristyle.** Built in 1907, this elegant neoclassical structure with massive Ionic columns originally served as a dance pavilion. Four concrete lions guard the structure, whose steps lead down to the bayou. There, you can watch the graceful swans and geese and ducks who shamelessly beg for food from passersby. The Peristyle continues to set the scene for countless weddings, cocktail parties, picnics, and, of course, outdoor dances. 🕐 *15 min. Dreyfous Dr. overlooking Bayou Metairie.*

⓬ **Popp Bandstand.** Erected in 1917, the bandstand remains popular for outdoor concerts. U.S. Marine bandleader John Philip Sousa performed here in 1928 and a live oak beside the bandstand was named in his honor. Unfortunately, the original Sousa Oak died in 1987. The Marines asked the Live Oak Society—of which all of the park's mature oaks are members in good standing—to name another oak for the famous American composer. The huge live oak to the left of the Peristyle is now known as the Sousa Oak. 🕐 *10 min. Dreyfous Dr. overlooking Bayou Metairie.*

⓭ **Fishing the Lagoons.** Unlike Uptown's Audubon Park, fishing is allowed in City Park's 11 miles (18km) of lagoons. In their shallow depths, you'll (hopefully!) catch bass, catfish, and perch. Freshwater fishing permits are required by the State of Louisiana Department of Wildlife and Fisheries and are available for purchase online or by phone (*www.wlf.state.la.us*; ☎ *888/765-2602*). ☎ *504/483-9371. www.new orleanscitypark.com. Fishing permit $9.50 (annual) resident, $5.00 (1 day) or $15 (4 days) nonresident, plus service fee if ordered online/by phone. Open daily sunrise–sunset.*

⓮ **Couterie Forest Arboretum.** More than 280 bird species, from egrets to water thrushes, make for a birder's paradise. The 30-acre (12-hectare) park features fishing, birding, and hiking. 🕐 *½–1 hr. Harrison Ave. at Diagonal Dr. turnaround. ☎ 504/482-4888. www.neworleanscitypark.com. Free admission. Open daily 8am–6pm.*

⓯ **Equest Farm.** This family-owned riding stable on 13 acres (5.2 hectares) offers horseback rides and English riding lessons. You must call ahead for a reservation. 🕐 *1 hr. 1001 Filmore Ave. ☎ 504/483-9398. www.equestfarm.com. English riding lesson fees $50 private half-hour, $45 per person semiprivate (2 riders) half-hour, $40 per person group (3–6 riders) 1 hr. Tues–Fri 8–9am and 4–7pm, Sat–Sun 8–11am and 4–7pm.*

Mississippi River

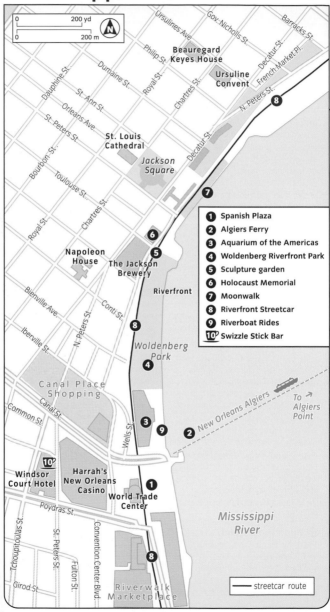

0   200 yd
0   200 m

Ursulines Ave.
Gov. Nicholls St.
Barracks St.
Philip St.
Dumaine St.
Dauphine St.
St. Ann St.
Orleans Ave.
St. Peters St.
Royal St.
Chartres St.
Decatur St.
French Market Pl.
N. Peters St.

Beauregard Keyes House

Ursuline Convent

St. Louis Cathedral

Jackson Square

Bourbon St.
Toulouse St.
Royal St.
Chartres St.

Napoleon House

The Jackson Brewery

Riverfront

Bienville Ave.
Conti St.
Iberville St.
N. Peters St.

Woldenberg Park

Canal Place Shopping

Common St.
Canal St.
Wells St.

New Orleans Algiers

To →
Algiers
Point

Windsor Court Hotel

Harrah's New Orleans Casino

World Trade Center

Poydras St.
Tchoupitoulas St.
St. Peters St.
Convention Center Blvd.
Fulton St.
Girod St.

Riverwalk Marketplace

Mississippi River

1. Spanish Plaza
2. Algiers Ferry
3. Aquarium of the Americas
4. Woldenberg Riverfront Park
5. Sculpture garden
6. Holocaust Memorial
7. Moonwalk
8. Riverfront Streetcar
9. Riverboat Rides
10. Swizzle Stick Bar

— streetcar route

New Orleans simply wouldn't exist without the Mississippi River. Early settlers recognized that the high ground tucked into a "crescent" of the river would make for a perfect international port so the original Crescent City—the French Quarter—was founded in 1718. Today, the riverfront remains a bustling public thoroughfare, offering sweeping views of the mythical waterway from land or ferry, and lush landscaping, statues, and sculpture along the walking path as birds and street musicians fill the humid air with song. START: **Spanish Plaza, 1 Poydras St.**

❶ Spanish Plaza. Perhaps one of the least known romantic spots in the city, this beautifully tiled fountain with a view of the Mississippi was given to the city during the U.S. bicentennial in 1976 as a gift from Spain. Occasionally, you'll see a couple get married here then disappear back into the French Quarter. ⏱ *20 min. 1 Poydras St. at Mississippi River, beside Riverwalk Mall. Free admission. Daily 10am–6pm.*

❷ Algiers Ferry. While not as old or architecturally pleasing as the other river ferry boats, this is the only one that's free and takes you across the river to Algiers Point, an historic neighborhood—bounded by Atlantic and Newton streets and the Mississippi—founded in 1719. ⏱ *15 min. Foot of Canal St.* ☎ *504/376-8180 or 504/363-9090. www.friendsoftheferry.org. Cars $1 (Algiers side only), pedestrian passengers free. Runs daily 6am–12:15am, leaves every 30 min.*

Tiles line the Spanish Plaza fountain.

Views of the Mississippi and St. Louis Cathedral from the Algiers ferry.

❸ kids Aquarium of the Americas. A shady bench at the sprawling entrance to the aquarium is a wonderful place to relax while the kids ooh and aah over the cute marine-life sculptures and real-life seagulls swooping in for crumbs.

See p. 47, **②** ⏱ *20 min.–3 hr. (if you go inside). 1 Canal St.*

④ Woldenberg Riverfront Park. The park, just under 20 acres, is named after local philanthropist and civic leader Malcolm Woldenberg. ⏱ *30 min. Along river btw. aquarium and Jackson Square. Free admission.*

⑤ Sculpture garden. This informal sculpture garden has grown in size and artistic importance over the decades. My favorite is Robert Schoen's Carrara marble figure, *Old Man River,* a fitting tribute to the breadth and depth of the Mississippi. ⏱ *30 min. Inside Woldenberg Park. Free admission.*

⑥ Holocaust Memorial. Dedicated in 2003, this inspiring memorial was rendered by Israeli artist and sculptor Yaacov Agam. ⏱ *15–30 min. Inside Woldenberg Park. Free admission.*

⑦ kids Moonwalk. The riverside path offers a scenic view of the Mississippi River and the Crescent City Connection. See p. 9, **①**. ⏱ *20 min. Across from Jackson Square along Mississippi River. Go before 8pm for safety's sake.*

⑧ Riverfront Streetcar. Cherry red, vintage-looking streetcars run nearly 2 miles (3.2km) along the river past old wharves and warehouses behind the French Market, giving you a glimpse of the glory days of river-run industry. ⏱ *20 min. Thalia St. to Esplanade Ave.* ☎ *504/248-3900. www.norta.com. Fare $1.25 one-way.*

⑨ kids Riverboat rides. Enjoy the city skyline on the Steamboat *Natchez,* one of only six steam-powered stern-wheelers on the Mississippi; or the New Orleans Paddlewheels Company's *Creole Queen* and *Cajun Queen.* Food and special dinner tours are available; save your money and dine elsewhere. ⏱ *2 hr. Docked near the end of Canal St. and the aquarium. Steamboat Natchez.* ☎ *504/586-8777. Admission $25 adult, $12 child. Cruises daily 11:30am–1:30pm and 2:30–4:30pm. New Orleans Paddlewheel Company.* ☎ *504/529-4567. Admission $25 adult, $13 child. Call for cruise days/times.*

❿ Swizzle Stick Bar. Stop in for a swanky end of tour cocktail at this hip and classy bar inside the Loews New Orleans Hotel. *300 Poydras St.,* ☎ *504/595-3305. $.* ●

The Creole Queen.

Dining Best Bets

Best **Celebrity-Chef Meal**
★★ Emeril's $$$ *800 Tchoupitoulas St. (p 104)*

Best **Creole Restaurant**
★★ Arnaud's $$$ *813 Bienville St. (p 101)*

Best **Comfort Food**
★★ Liuzza's on Bienville $ *3636 Bienville St. (p 106)*

Best **Diner**
★ Mother's $ *401 Poydras St. (p 106)*

Best **Burger**
★ **Port of Call** $ *838 Esplanade Ave. (p 107)*

Best **Fried Chicken**
★ Willie Mae's Scotch House $ *2401 St. Ann St. (p 108)*

Best **Bakery**
★★ Croissant D'Or $ *617 Ursulines St. (p 103)*

Best **Creole/Acadian Restaurant**
★★★ Brigtsen's $$ *723 Dante St. (p 102)*

Most **Worth the Wait**
★★ Irene's Cuisine $ *539 St. Philip St. (p 106)*

Most **Romantic**
★★★ Upperline $$ *1413 Upperline St. (p 108)*

Best **Breakfast**
★★★ Elizabeth's $$ *601 Gallier St. (p 104)*

Best **Neighborhood Italian**
★★ Liuzza's on Bienville $ *3636 Bienville St. (p 106)*

Best **Po' Boy**
★★ Guy's $ *5259 Magazine St. (p 105)*

Best **Place to Find Locals**
★ Riccobono's Panola Street Café $, *7801 Panola St. (p 108)*

Best **New Southern**
★★★ Dick & Jenny's $$ *4501 Tchoupitoulas St. (p 104)*

Best **Jazz Brunch**
★★ Palace Café $$, *605 Canal St. (p 107)*

Best **Four-Star Meal at Two-Star Prices**
★★ Ciro's Cote Sud $$ *7918 Maple St. (p 103)*

Best **Ice Cream**
★★★ The Creole Creamery $ *4924 Prytania St. (p 103)*

Best **Burrito**
★★ Taqueria Corona $ *5932 Magazine St. (p 108)*

Best **Meal in a Truckbed**
★★★ Jacques-Imo's $$ *8324 Oak St. (p 106)*

French Quarter Dining

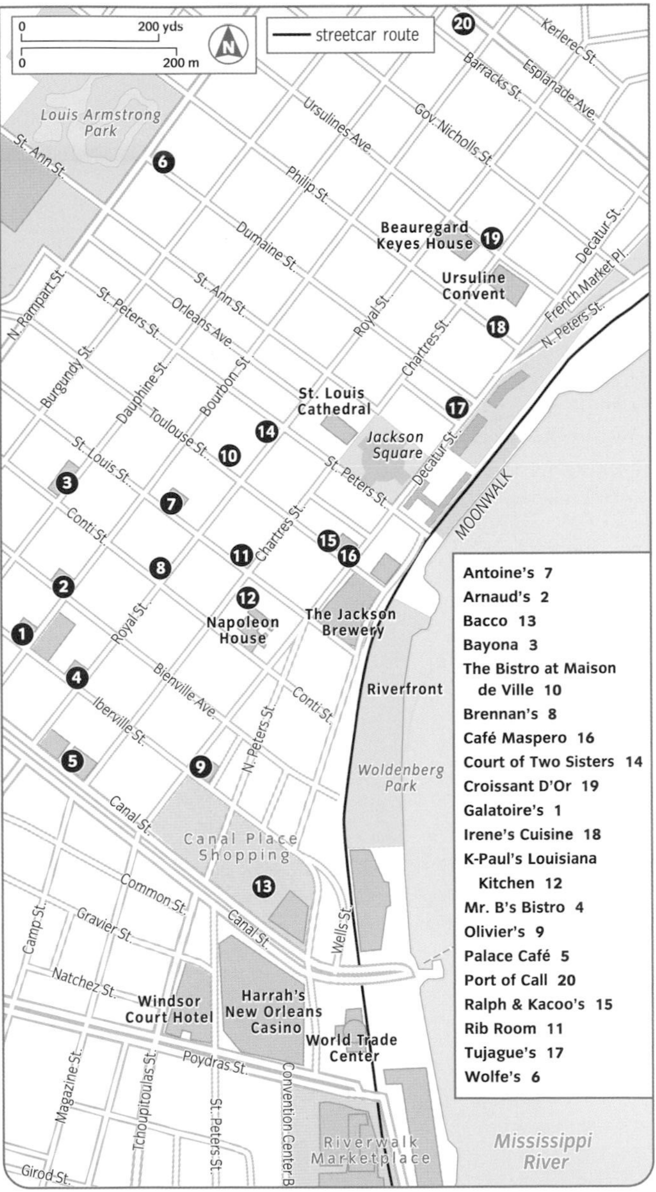
0 200 yds
0 200 m
N
streetcar route
Louis Armstrong Park
St. Ann St.
Kerlerec St.
Esplanade Ave.
Barracks St.
Gov. Nicholls St.
Ursulines Ave.
Philip St.
Dumaine St.
St. Ann St.
Orleans Ave.
St. Peters St.
Toulouse St.
St. Louis St.
Conti St.
Bienville Ave.
Iberville St.
Canal St.
Common St.
Gravier St.
Natchez St.
Poydras St.
Girod St.
N. Rampart St.
Burgundy St.
Dauphine St.
Bourbon St.
Royal St.
Chartres St.
Decatur St.
French Market Pl.
N. Peters St.
Wells St.
Camp St.
Magazine St.
Tchoupitoulas St.
St. Peters St.
Convention Center B
Beauregard Keyes House
Ursuline Convent
St. Louis Cathedral
Jackson Square
MOONWALK
Napoleon House
The Jackson Brewery
Riverfront
Woldenberg Park
Canal Place Shopping
Windsor Court Hotel
Harrah's New Orleans Casino
World Trade Center
Riverwalk Marketplace
Mississippi River
Antoine's 7
Arnaud's 2
Bacco 13
Bayona 3
The Bistro at Maison de Ville 10
Brennan's 8
Café Maspero 16
Court of Two Sisters 14
Croissant D'Or 19
Galatoire's 1
Irene's Cuisine 18
K-Paul's Louisiana Kitchen 12
Mr. B's Bistro 4
Olivier's 9
Palace Café 5
Port of Call 20
Ralph & Kacoo's 15
Rib Room 11
Tujague's 17
Wolfe's 6

Central Business District Dining

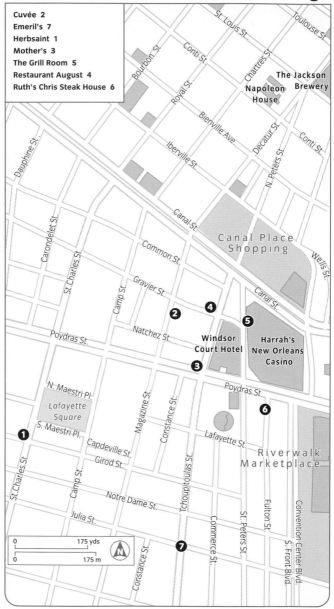

Cuvée 2
Emeril's 7
Herbsaint 1
Mother's 3
The Grill Room 5
Restaurant August 4
Ruth's Chris Steak House 6

Uptown Dining

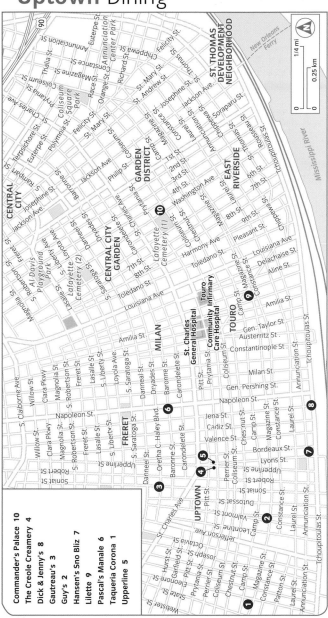

Commander's Palace 10
The Creole Creamery 4
Dick & Jenny's 8
Gautreau's 3
Guy's 2
Hansen's Sno Bliz 7
Lilette 9
Pascal's Manale 6
Taqueria Corona 1
Upperline 5

Carrollton/Mid-City Dining

Brigtsen's **2**
Ciro's Cote Sud **1**
Dooky Chase **8**
Jacques-Imo's Café **3**
Liuzza's on Bienville **6**
Ralph's on the Park **5**
Riccobono's Panola
Street Café **4**
Willie Mae's Scotch House **7**

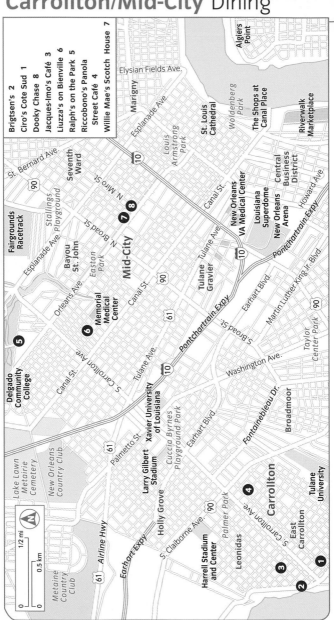

Dining A to Z

★ Antoine's FRENCH QUARTER *FRENCH/CREOLE* A truly original mom 'n' pop–type restaurant, Antoine's has evolved into one of New Orleans' most lauded and popular upscale establishments under the guidance of the same family for more than 160 years. Start with oysters Rockefeller and finish with the flashy baked Alaska; you can't go wrong with anything in between. *713 St. Louis St.* ☎ *504/581-4422. www.antoines.com. Reservations recommended. Jackets required for dinner. Entrees $22–$56 (most under $25). AE, DC, MC, V. Lunch & dinner Mon–Sat, brunch Sun. Map p 97.*

Antoine's famous baked Alaska.

★★ Arnaud's FRENCH QUARTER *CREOLE* The history of a culture haunts you like a specter here, from the moody antique lighting to the dark, butter-rich sauces on every plate. Expect traditional crab cakes and shrimp Creole, as well as fantastic fish dishes and top-notch steaks. Dare to venture up the creaky stairs for a peek at founder Germaine Wells's early-19th-century haute Carnival couture. *813 Bienville St.* ☎ *866/230-8895 or 504/523-5433. www.arnauds.com. Reservations recommended. Jackets required for dinner. Entrees $19–$38. AE, DC, DISC, MC, V. Dinner daily, jazz brunch Sun. Map p 97.*

★ Bacco FRENCH QUARTER *CREOLE/ ITALIAN* One of the younger Brennan family restaurants balances Italian comfort food with creative Creole accents. *310 Chartres St.* ☎ *504/522-2426. www.bacco.com. Reservations recommended. Entrees $15–$31. AE, DC, MC, V. Lunch & dinner daily 11:30am–2pm and 6–10 pm. Map p 97.*

★★★ Bayona FRENCH QUARTER *INTERNATIONAL* For nearly 20 years, chef-owner Susan Spicer

Arnaud's Carnival couture collection.

tempts the bravest of palates in a romantic 200-year-old Creole cottage setting. She prepares local sense-surprising seafood riches like crawfish, shrimp, and redfish, with an international flair. Bayona's name reflects the original Spanish name for Dauphine Street, *Camino de Bayona*. *430 Dauphine St.* ☎ *504/525-4455. www.bayona.com. Reservations required for dinner. Entrees $24–$28. AE, DC, DISC, MC, V. Lunch Mon–Fri, dinner Mon–Sat. Map p 97.*

The Bistro at Maison de Ville

FRENCH QUARTER *INTERNATIONAL* Popular among theater crowds and Francophiles who appreciate the Parisian-style decor and elegant interpretations of Louisiana Creole dishes (no Zatarain's here!). Prepare to wait a good while and, once seated, possibly knock knees with your tablemates. *733 Toulouse St. (in the Hotel Maison de Ville).* ☎ *504/ 528-9206. www.maisondeville.com. Reservations recommended. Entrees $29–$39. AE, DC, DISC, MC, V. Lunch daily, dinner Thurs–Sat. Map p 97.*

Brennan's FRENCH QUARTER

CREOLE/FRENCH Breakfast at Brennan's is indulgent and satisfying, although your $50 will go farther (and you'll have more breathing

A server heats things up at Brennan's.

Chef Frank Brigtsen.

room) if you come for lunch or dinner instead. *417 Royal St.* ☎ *504/525-9711. www.brennansneworleans. com. Reservations recommended. Entrees $15–$20 breakfast, $35 for 3-course prix-fixe breakfast; dinner $29–$39. AE, DC, DISC, MC, V. Breakfast, lunch & dinner daily. Map p 97.*

★★★ Brigtsen's CARROLLTON

CREOLE/ACADIAN The moment you step inside this tucked away 19th-century Victorian cottage, hostess Marna Brigtsen will make you feel at home. Chef Frank Brigtsen insists on seasonal, fresh food produced locally whenever possible; your taste buds can tell the difference. When in season, order the seafood platter, piled high with drum, shrimp, crawfish, oysters, and scallops. *723 Dante St.* ☎ *504/861-7610. www.brigtsens. com. Reservations required. Entrees $19–$28. AE, DC, MC, V. Dinner Tues–Sat. Map p 100.*

kids Café Maspero FRENCH

QUARTER *SANDWICHES/SEAFOOD* Perhaps the only sandwich place I know that doesn't serve po' boys, but the familiar finger food is fun for little ones. *601 Decatur St.* ☎ *504/ 523-6250. Entrees $4.25–$9. Lunch & dinner daily. Map p 96.*

★★ Ciro's Cote Sud CARROLL-
TON *FRENCH/PIZZA* When a
French chef buys an Italian pizza
parlor you get sinfully rich provincial
French fare and thin-crust pizza on
the same menu. Skip the 'za and go
for the shrimp, Louisiana crawfish
tails, and scallops in a creamy curry
sauce. Spicy and smooth all in one
forkful. *7918 Maple St.* ☎ *504/866-
9551. www.cotesudrestaurant.com.
Entrees $11–$22. No credit cards.
Dinner nightly. Map p 100.*

★★★ Commander's Palace
GARDEN DISTRICT *CREOLE* The
Brennan family is known for spotting talent—legendary chefs Paul
Prudhomme, Emeril Lagasse, and
Jamie Shannon all got their start
here—so it's no surprise that
30-year-old executive chef Tory
McPhail is a James Beard Rising Star
Chef Nominee. The first time I ever
experienced soft shell crab was
here, and it remains the most ten-
der, flavorful seafood I've ever
tasted. *1403 Washington Ave.*
☎ *504/899-8221. www.commanders
palace.com. Upscale dress, jackets
preferred at dinner; no shorts.
Entrees $36–$45, brunch $27–$32.
Lunch Mon–Fri, dinner nightly,
brunch Sat–Sun. Map p 99.*

kids Court of Two Sisters
FRENCH QUARTER *CREOLE* The
exposed brick, soothing fountain
and jazz music add up to a stronger
impression than the food, which
includes takes on Creole-style fish,
fowl, and beef. Reasonably
priced children's menu
available. *613 Royal
St.* ☎ *504/522-
7261. www.court
oftwosisters.com.
Reservations
recommended.
Entrees $25–$35,
brunch $25. AE, DC,
DISC, MC, V. Brunch & dinner
daily. Map p 97.*

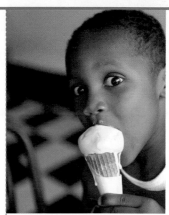

*There's a flavor for everyone at the
Creole Creamery.*

**★★★ kids The Creole Cream-
ery** UPTOWN *ICE CREAM* This
neighborhood ice cream parlor looks
like a throwback to the 1950s but
boasts totally modern taste combinations. Have you ever tried flavors like
lavender honey, red velvet cake, or
Mexican hot chocolate? If you can't
decide, choose four or six mini-
scoops for an ice cream sampler.
4924 Prytania St. ☎ *504/894-8680.
www.creolecreamery.com. 1 scoop
$2.50, sundaes $4.25–$6.50. No credit
cards. Open noon–10pm Sun–Thurs,
noon–11pm Fri–Sat. Map p 99.*

★★ Croissant D'Or FRENCH
QUARTER *SANDWICHES/PASTRIES*
Almost every Sunday, we meet
friends at this quiet French bakery
to sip delicious iced coffee and
munch flaky choco-
late croissants, mini
apple tarts,
quiche, and
crunchy tuna
salad sand-
wiches. *617
Ursulines St.*
☎ *504/524-4663.*

Croissant d'or

The sign outside the Croissant D'Or.

Softshell crab at Dick & Jenny's.

Entrees $8 and under. AE, MC, V.
Breakfast & lunch Wed–Sun. Map
p 97.

★ **Cuvée** CENTRAL BUSINESS DIS-
TRICT *CREOLE/NEW AMERICAN*
Cuvée offers a fresh take on contemporary French cuisine in an intimate setting gently lit by antique
gas lamps. *322 Magazine St. ☎ 504/
587-9001. www.restaurantcuvee.
com. Reservations recommended.
Entrees $18–$28. AE, DC, MC, V.
Dinner Mon–Sat. Map p 98.*

★★★ **Dick & Jenny's** UPTOWN
CREOLE/ECLECTIC The slow-food
revolution meets youthful vitality.

Elizabeth's praline bacon.

Dishes such as ginger crusted
salmon and stuffed pork tenderloin
are absolutely worth the wait. *4501
Tchoupitoulas St. ☎ 504/894-9880.
No reservations available. Entrees
$14–$23. AE, DISC, MC, V. Dinner
Tues–Sat. Map p 99.*

Dooky Chase TREME *CREOLE/
SOUL FOOD* Upscale soul food
from octogenarian chef-matriarch
Leah Chase is only available for
take-out and lunch. Let's hope it'll
soon open for dinner again. *2301
Orleans Ave. ☎ 504/821-0600.
Entrees $12–$20. No credit cards.
Take-out or lunch only Tues–Thurs.
Map p 100.*

★★★ **Elizabeth's** BYWATER
BREAKFAST/CREOLE Yeah, it's out
of the way, but I'd drive hundreds of
miles for its sweet, crispy praline
bacon. *601 Gallier St. ☎ 504/944-
9272. www.elizabeths-restaurant.
com. Entrees $10–$25. MC, V. Lunch
& dinner Tues–Fri, brunch Sat–Sun.*

★★ **Emeril's** CENTRAL BUSINESS
DISTRICT *CREOLE/NEW AMERICAN*
Who doesn't know the "Bam" man?
His star has fallen a bit from overex-
posure but when he's in the kitchen,
the food and service are all kicked
up a notch. *800 Tchoupitoulas St.*

Preparing the po'boys at Guy's.

☎ 504/528-9393. www.emerils.com. Reservations required. Entrees $26–$39; 7-course degustation menu (changes nightly) $65. AE, DC, DISC, MC, V. Lunch Mon–Fri, dinner daily. Map p 98.

★★ **Galatoire's** FRENCH QUARTER *FRENCH*   Grab Tennessee Williams's table (in the main window, in front of the word "Restaurant") and prepare to be satiated by extravagant, multi-course French meals prepared from recipes that have been in the family since 1905. *209 Bourbon St.* ☎ *504/525-2021. www.galatoires.com. Reservations accepted for 2nd-floor dining room only. Jackets required for dinner and on Sun. Entrees $14–$27. AE, DC, DISC, MC, V. Lunch & dinner Tues–Sun. Map p 97.*

★★ **Gautreau's** UPTOWN *MODERN FRENCH/LOUISIANA*   The flickering candlelight, Parisian-style *trompe l'oeil* on the walls, and tin ceiling set a romantic mood in this brilliantly converted neighborhood drugstore. (You can still see the original antique apothecary cases, which now display wine and liquor.) The menu changes every 6 weeks to take advantage of seasonal seafood and produce. *1728 Soniat St.* ☎ *504/899-7397. www.gautreausrestaurant. com. Reservations recommended.*

Entrees $22–$35. AE, MC, V. Dinner Mon–Sat. Map p 99.

★★ **The Grill Room** CENTRAL BUSINESS DISTRICT *INTERNATIONAL* Indulgent without being excessive. Delights include lump crab cakes, Colorado lamb chops, and seared diver scallops. *300 Gravier St.* ☎ *504/522-1992. www.windsorcourthotel.com. Reservations recommended. Entrees $28–$39. AE, DC, DISC, MC, V. Breakfast, lunch & dinner daily, brunch Sun. Map p 98.*

★★ **Guy's** UPTOWN *SANDWICHES* Guy will make you the best grilled shrimp po' boy you've ever had. Be sure to grab lots of napkins because that fresh French bread can only soak up so much buttery juice. *5259 Magazine St.* ☎ *504/891-5025. Sandwiches $4.50–$11. No credit cards. Lunch Mon–Sat. Map p 99.*

★★ **Hansen's Sno Bliz** UPTOWN *SHAVED ICE*   Ernest and Mary Hansen founded this family favorite back in 1939; their granddaughter Ashley continues to run it today. Ernest's snowball machine invention creates such finely shaved ice that it's like eating snowflakes. While waiting in line, check out the fun wall of photos of past patrons. *4801 Tchoupitoulas St.* ☎ *504/891-9788.*

www.snobliz.com. Cash only. Mon–Sat 1–7pm, closed Sun. Map p 99.

★ **Herbsaint** CENTRAL BUSINESS DISTRICT *FRENCH/NEW AMERICAN* Chef-owner Donald Link offers hearty Southern comfort food such as pork belly, gumbo, okra, and collard greens in a casual bistro setting. *701 St. Charles Ave. ☎ 504/524-4114. www.herbsaint.com. Reservations recommended. Entrees $14–$24. AE, DC, DISC, MC, V. Lunch Mon–Fri, dinner Mon–Sat. Map p 98.*

★★ **Irene's Cuisine** FRENCH QUARTER *FRENCH/ITALIAN* Good things come to those who wait, namely a fine Italian meal, mood-altering desserts, and brisk service. Despite plenty of competition, oyster lovers claim its charbroiled oysters topped with melted cheese and bits of bacon are the best in the city. *539 St. Philip St. ☎ 504/529-8811. Reservations not accepted (except for holidays). Entrees $14–$18. AE, MC, V. Dinner nightly. Map p 97.*

★★★ **Jacques-Imo's Café** CARROLLTON *CREOLE/SOUL FOOD* Enjoy your stuffed pork chop or fried chicken seated in the truck parked outside and be the envy of all. *8324 Oak St. ☎ 504/861-0886. www.jacquesimoscafe.com. Reservations accepted for parties of 5 or more. Entrees $17–$25. AE, DC, DISC, MC, V. Dinner Mon–Sat. Map p 100.*

★★ **K-Paul's Louisiana Kitchen** FRENCH QUARTER *CAJUN* Chef-owner Paul Prudhomme's signature blackened redfish remains a favorite even if it's gone mainstream. You'll eat well but pay way too much. *416 Chartres St. ☎ 504/524-7394. www.kpauls.com. Reservations recommended. Entrees $30–$40. AE, DC, DISC, MC, V. Lunch Thurs–Sat, dinner Mon–Sat. Map p 97.*

★ **Lilette** UPTOWN *CREOLE/FRENCH* Classic French fare meets experimental Creole flair in a cozy corner bistro. *3637 Magazine St. ☎ 504/895-1636. www.liletterestaurant.com. Reservations recommended. Entrees $18–$30. AE, DISC, MC, V. Lunch & dinner Tues–Sat. Map p 99.*

★★ **kids Liuzza's on Bienville** MID-CITY *ITALIAN/SANDWICHES/SEAFOOD* Locals have loved the simple comfort food here—including pastas, salads, and sandwiches—since 1947. *3636 Bienville St. ☎ 504/482-9120. www.liuzzas.com. Entrees $10–$20. No credit cards. Lunch & dinner Tues–Sat. Map p 100.*

★ **kids Mother's** CENTRAL BUSINESS DISTRICT *BREAKFAST/CREOLE/SANDWICHES/SHORT ORDER* Nothing fancy just really good, greasy diner food. *401 Poydras St. ☎ 504/523-9656. www.mothersrestaurant.net. Entrees $9–$20. AE, DISC, MC,*

Dinner in the truck at Jacques-Imo's.

V. Breakfast, lunch & dinner daily. Map p 98.

Mr. B's Bistro FRENCH QUARTER *CONTEMPORARY CREOLE* A Brennan family favorite among businesspeople and politicians brokering lunchtime deals. The crab cakes and Gumbo Ya-Ya are excellent. *201 Royal St.* ☎ 504/523-2078. www.mrbsbistro.com. Entrees $24–$42. AE, DC, DISC, MC, V. Lunch Mon–Sat, dinner nightly, jazz brunch Sun. Map p 97.

★ **Olivier's** FRENCH QUARTER *CREOLE/FRENCH* Old-fashioned family cooking is in Chef Armand Olivier's blood. Some of his recipes—such as Creole rabbit and crawfish étoufée—have been passed down through generations. *204 Decatur St.* ☎ 504/525-7734. www.olivierscreole.com. Reservations recommended. Entrees $16–$22. AE, DC, DISC, MC, V. Dinner Thurs–Tues. Map p 97.

★★ **Palace Café** FRENCH QUARTER *CONTEMPORARY CREOLE* Part of the Brennan family of restaurants, Palace Café offers creative takes on seafood, pork, and other seasonal specialties. And for dessert? I have four words for you: white chocolate bread pudding. You're welcome. *605 Canal St.* ☎ 504/523-1661. www.palacecafe.com. Reservations recommended. Entrees $20–$32. AE, DC, DISC, MC, V. Lunch Mon–Fri, dinner nightly, jazz brunch Sat–Sun. Map p 97.

Pascal's Manale UPTOWN *ITALIAN/SEAFOOD/STEAKHOUSE* Skip the steak and go for the barbecued shrimp and raw oysters. *1838 Napoleon Ave.* ☎ 504/895-4877. Reservations recommended. Entrees $15–$32. AE, DC, DISC, MC, V. Lunch Wed–Fri, dinner Mon–Sat. Map p 99.

★ **Port of Call** FRENCH QUARTER *HAMBURGERS/SANDWICHES* If you're going to eat a burger in New Orleans, this is the place to get it.

Onion rings and a cold one at Liuzza's.

838 Esplanade Ave. ☎ 504/523-0120. www.portofcallneworleans.com. Entrees $8–$21. AE, MC, V. Lunch & dinner daily. Map p 97.

kids Ralph & Kacoo's FRENCH QUARTER *CREOLE/SEAFOOD* Huge portions and decent prices make this chain—serving fried crawfish, onion rings, oysters, and the like—better than some. *519 Toulouse St.* ☎ 504/522-5226. www.ralphandkacoos.com. Reservations recommended. Entrees $14–$40. AE, DC, DISC, MC, V. Lunch Sat–Sun, dinner nightly. Map p 97.

★ **Ralph's on the Park** MID-CITY *CREOLE/SEAFOOD* Lovely view of City Park's giant oaks in an historic neighborhood. Oh, and the food, which includes braised lamb, crawfish salad, and baked oysters Ralph, is good, too. *900 City Park Ave.* ☎ 504/488-1000. www.ralphsonthepark.com. Reservations recommended. Entrees $18–$40. AE, MC, V. Lunch Fri, dinner Tues–Sat, brunch Sun. Map p 100.

★★★ **Restaurant August** CENTRAL BUSINESS DISTRICT *CONTEMPORARY FRENCH* Executive chef John Besh applies his native Louisiana instincts to signature French dishes. *301 Tchoupitoulas St.* ☎ 504/299-9777. www.rest-august.com. Reservations recommended. Entrees $22–$40. AE, DC, MC, V. Lunch Fri, dinner Tues–Sat. Map p 98.

Rib Room FRENCH QUARTER *SEA-FOOD/STEAKHOUSE* Sometimes you just need the simple perfection of prime rib. *621 St. Louis St. ☎ 504/529-7045. www.omniroyalorleans. com. Reservations recommended. Entrees $24–$36. AE, DC, DISC, MC, V. Breakfast, lunch & dinner daily. Map p 97.*

★ **kids** **Riccobono's Panola Street Café** CARROLLTON *BREAK-FAST/SANDWICHES* Welcome to a true neighborhood hangout, where locals gather with family and friends to catch up over free coffee refills, eggs made any way you like 'em, and the usual breakfast staples of sausage, bacon, and biscuits. (Breakfast served all day.) The college student servers give you quick, attentive service. *7801 Panola St. ☎ 504/314-1810. Entrees $7–$20. AE, MC, V. Breakfast & lunch daily. Map p 100.*

★★ **kids** **Taqueria Corona** UPTOWN *MEXICAN* Coeds, Uptown families, suburbanites, and tourists all come here for the cheap, plentiful, goof food. Start with crispy hot chips, tangy pico de gallo, and a margarita. For a taste of everything at a ridiculously good price, choose one of the combination platters. *5932 Magazine St. ☎ 504/897-3974. http://taqueria corona.com. Entrees $8–$15. Lunch & dinner daily. Map p 99.*

★ **Tujague's** FRENCH QUARTER *CREOLE* Old-fashioned and set in its ways; what do you expect from a restaurant dating back to 1856? Beef brisket and shrimp rémoulade are typical offerings. *823 Decatur St. ☎ 504/525-8676. www.tujagues restaurant.com. Reservations recommended. 6 courses $30–$38. AE, DC, DISC, MC, V. Dinner nightly. Map p 97.*

★★★ **Upperline** UPTOWN *CREOLE/ECLECTIC* Owner-hostess JoAnn Clevenger makes a point of visiting

Upperline restaurant.

every table to chat with diners, so do your best to tear yourself away from those fried green tomatoes topped with tangy shrimp rémoulade. *1413 Upperline St. ☎ 504/891-9822. www. upperline.com. Reservations required. Entrees $20–$27. AE, DC, MC, V. Dinner Wed–Sun. Map p 99.*

★ **Willie Mae's Scotch House** MID-CITY *SOUL FOOD* Sink your teeth into the juicy, fried chicken served with a side of creamy butter beans. *2401 St. Ann St. ☎ 504/822-9503. Everything under $15. No credit cards. Lunch daily. Map p 100.*

Wolfe's FRENCH QUARTER *FRENCH/ITALIAN/NEW AMERICAN* Chef Tom Wolfe takes risks with his menu, but I can never resist the staple Gulf fish amandine, pan-seared drum with toasted almond beurre noisette, wilted leek potato hash, and garlic sautéed kale. *1041 Dumaine St. ☎ 504/593-9535. www.wolfes restaurant.com. Reservations recommended. Entrees $18–$35. AE, DC, MC, V. Lunch Fri, dinner Tues–Sat. Map p 97. ●*

Nightlife Best Bets

Irvin Mayfield performs at Snug Harbor.

Best Burlesque
★ One Eyed Jacks, *615 Toulouse St. (p 119)*

Best Happy Hour
★ Razzoo, *511 Bourbon St. (p 118)*

Best Dive Bar
★ Snake & Jake's Xmas Club Lounge, *7612 Oak St. (p 116)*

Best Late-Late Spot
★ The Dungeon, *738 Toulouse St. (p 119)*

Best Gay & Lesbian
★★★ Oz, *800 Bourbon St. (p 118)*

Best Downtown Bar
★★ Ampersand, *1100 Tulane Ave. (p 118)*

Best Cajun Dancing
★ Mulate's, *201 Julia St. (p 117)*

Best Historic Bar
★★ Napoleon House, *500 Chartres St. (p 120)*

Best Karaoke
★ Cat's Meow, *701 Bourbon St. (p 121)*

Best Jazz Club
★★ Snug Harbor, *626 Frenchmen St. (p 120)*

Best Jukebox
★ F&M Patio Bar, *4841 Tchoupitoulas St. (p 119)*

Previous page: A bartender at Molly's at the Market pours a local favorite, Abita Springs beer.

French Quarter Nightlife

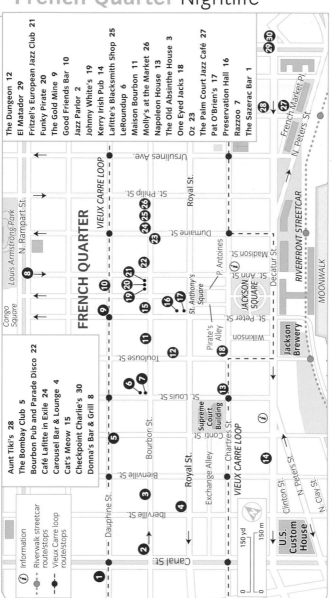

The Dungeon 12
El Matador 29
Fritzel's European Jazz Club 21
Funky Pirate 20
The Gold Mine 9
Good Friends Bar 10
Jazz Parlor 2
Johnny White's 19
Kerry Irish Pub 14
Lafitte's Blacksmith Shop 25
LeRoundup 6
Maison Bourbon 11
Molly's at the Market 26
Napoleon House 13
The Old Absinthe House 3
One Eyed Jacks 18
Oz 23
The Palm Court Jazz Café 27
Pat O'Brien's 17
Preservation Hall 16
Razzoo 7
The Sazerac Bar 1

Aunt Tiki's 28
The Bombay Club 5
Bourbon Pub and Parade Disco 22
Café Lafitte in Exile 24
Carousel Bar & Lounge 4
Cat's Meow 15
Checkpoint Charlie's 30
Donna's Bar & Grill 8

FRENCH QUARTER

i Information
Riverwalk streetcar route/stops
Vieux Carre loop route/stops

Uptown Nightlife

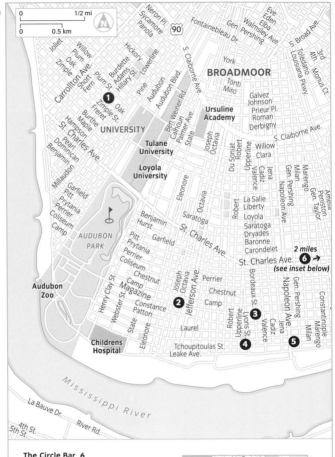

The Circle Bar 6

F&M Patio Bar 4

Le Bon Temps Roulé 3

St. Joe's Bar 2

Snake & Jake's Xmas Club Lounge 1

Tipitina's 5

Central Business District
Nightlife

Ampersand **1**
The Howlin' Wolf **3**
Michaul's on St. Charles **2**
Mulate's **4**

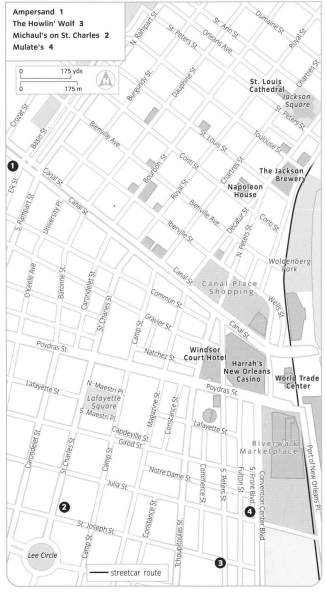

Fauberg Marigny/Bywater
Nightlife

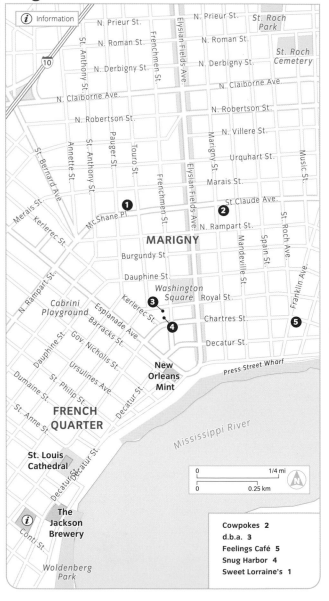

Cowpokes **2**
d.b.a. **3**
Feelings Café **5**
Snug Harbor **4**
Sweet Lorraine's **1**

Carrollton/Mid-City Nightlife

Carrollton Station 3
Cooter Brown's Tavern 1
The Maple Leaf 2

Nightlife A to Z

Bars

Aunt Tiki's FRENCH QUARTER
Like the name suggests, this is a good place to blend in with an eclectic crowd and the no-frills decor means you won't be gouged for drinks like at some Quarter establishments. *1207 Decatur St.* ☎ *504/680-8454. No cover. Map p 111.*

Johnny White's FRENCH QUARTER Open 24/7 no matter what (even Katrina). If you want to keep good company in a crisis, you'll find it here along with decent bar food thanks to its neighboring Cajun-American restaurant. *720 Bourbon St.* ☎ *504/524-4909. No cover. Map p 111.*

Le Bon Temps Roulé UPTOWN
Be prepared for a party crowd of coeds and neighborhood regulars who know how to pass a good time drinking Abita with greasy burgers and jamming to popular local acts on the weekends. *4801 Magazine St.* ☎ *504/895-8117. No cover. Map p 112.*

★★★ The Maple Leaf CARROLL-TON   Though small, the patio out back gives you a little breathing room and dancing space, which you'll definitely need if regular favorites BeauSoleil or Rebirth Brass Band are playing. College kids can run amok, but you'll find their profs here, too, more often than not. *8316*

Aunt Tiki's, a comfortable, no-frills bar in the French Quarter.

Oak St. ☎ 504/866-9359. Cover $5–$15. Map p 115.

★ Molly's at the Market

FRENCH QUARTER   You'll get the local scoop any night of the week thanks to a bizarre though typically New Orleans blend of patrons who always have a story to tell. *1107 Decatur St.* ☎ *504/525-5169. No cover. Map p 111.*

St. Joe's Bar UPTOWN   After a day of shopping on Magazine Street, relax at the dark, narrow bar or head back to a seat on the tropical patio; either way, you'll get attentive service and a little room to kick back—that is unless it's super late on the weekend and overrun by college kids and single 20-somethings. *5535 Magazine St.* ☎ *504/899-3744. No cover. Map p 112.*

★ Snake & Jake's Xmas Club Lounge

CARROLLTON   Only venture here if you like Christmas decorations year-round, dogs hanging out at their masters' feet, soul and R & B pumping from the jukebox, and really, really dark corners. *7612 Oak St.* ☎ *504/861-2802. No cover. Map p 112.*

★★★ Tipitina's

UPTOWN   I will never, ever forgive my college roommate for going to a show here without me and spotting Bono in the audience. No matter what music genre gets you off your feet—folk, rock, country, R & B—you'll find it here and occasionally, a famous face in the crowd. I prefer the balcony for people-watching and dancing because there's more room to groove. Learn to eat and dance like a Cajun at the free "Fais Do Do" every Sunday afternoon. *501 Napoleon Ave.* ☎ *504/895-8477 or* ☎ *504/ 897-3943. www.tipitinas.com. Cover $5–15. Map p 112.*

The crowd dances to Rebirth Brass Band at the Maple Leaf.

Patrons whoop it up at Molly's at the Market.

Blues Bars

Funky Pirate FRENCH QUARTER   Passionate blues lovers flock here for Chicago-style musings, often belted out by blues king Big Al Carson, who plays here most nights to a good-size but not rambunctious crowd. *727 Bourbon St. ☎ 504/523-1960. No cover. One-drink minimum. Map p 111.*

Cajun/Zydeco Venues

kids Michaul's on St. Charles CENTRAL BUSINESS DISTRICT   On the downside, Michaul's caters more to conventioneers and the decor has a banquet hall feel, but on the plus side, enjoy free Cajun dance lessons, live music, and boatloads of spicy crawfish. *840 St. Charles Ave. ☎ 800/563-4055 or 504/522-5517. www.michauls.com. No cover. Map p 113.*

★★★ Mid-City Lanes Rock 'n' Bowl MID-CITY   You can't be a guest at my house and not come here to experience one of New Orleans' more bizarre offerings—bowling and dancing to live Cajun and Zydeco music. **Note:** The owner plans to open a new location about a mile away (still on Carrollton), heading toward the river. No word yet on whether the down 'n' dirty original will close. *3000 S. Carrollton Ave. ☎ 504/861-1700. www.rock andbowl.com. Shoe rental $1. Lane rental $15/hr. Map p 3.*

★ Mulate's CENTRAL BUSINESS DISTRICT   Owner Kerry Boutté—born in the small Cajun town of Arnaudville—opened this popular New Orleans location nearly 30 years ago to bring live Cajun music, dancing, and food to the masses. It's the next best thing if you can't travel to Lafayette to experience the real deal. *201 Julia St. ☎ 504/522-1492. www.mulates.com. No cover. Map p 113.*

Dance Clubs

The Gold Mine FRENCH QUARTER   Under-30 hipsters work up a sweat to emo, techno, and whatever's popular, usually followed by a sweet flaming Dr. Pepper shot for extra energy. Poetry readings are held Thursday nights. *701 Dauphine St. ☎ 504/586-0745. Cover $5. Map p 111.*

Tipitina's.

Funky Pirate.

★ **Razzoo** FRENCH QUARTER Hey Razzoo, Pat O's wants its flaming fountain back! Imitation is the best form of flattery, but no one comes close to this club's dance floor, which is packed nightly with locals, students, and tourists shakin' their thing. *511 Bourbon St.* ☎ *504/522-5100. www.razzoo.com. No cover. Map p 111.*

Gay/Lesbian Bars

Bourbon Pub and Parade Disco FRENCH QUARTER One of the country's largest gay clubs boasts a downstairs bar blaring dance music and videos 24/7, but if you have disco fever and an urge to dress up in tight, colorful costumes, head upstairs to show off the hustle, bus stop, four corners, the bump, and more classic moves. *801 Bourbon St.* ☎ *504/529-2107. Cover $5–$10 weekends only. Map p 111.*

Café Lafitte in Exile FRENCH QUARTER Former Lafitte's Blacksmith Shop owner Tom Caplinger opened this legendary gay gathering spot that drew Tennessee Williams as a regular; open 24 hours.

901 Bourbon St. ☎ *504/522-8397. www.lafittes.com. No cover. Map p 111.*

Cowpokes BYWATER If you're a little bit country, don your best denim and leather duds and take a cab to this out-of-the-way watering hole to meet fellow urban cowboys. *2240 St. Claude Ave.* ☎ *504/947-0505. No cover. Map p 111.*

Good Friends Bar FRENCH QUARTER The attractive, friendly staff will make you feel at home and after a frozen Separator—brandy, milk, and coffee liqueur mixed with Kahlua ice cream—(or two), you'll want to join the group around the corner piano singing old favorites karaoke style. *740 Dauphine St.* ☎ *504/566-7191. www.goodfriends bar.com. No cover. Map p 111.*

LeRoundup FRENCH QUARTER Drag queens, transsexuals, hot men, bad boys—they're all here and ready to party. If you're shy, you won't be for long. *819 St. Louis St.* ☎ *504/561-8340. Cover $2–$5. Map p 111.*

★★★ **Oz** FRENCH QUARTER Anything goes here among the city's hottest, most muscled, best costumed men I've ever seen. They show off hip-swiveling moves that will make you blush or want to join in the naughty fun. *800 Bourbon St.* ☎ *877/599-8200 or 504/592-8200. www.ozneworleans.com. Cover $3–$10. Map p 111.*

Hip Spots

★★ **Ampersand** CENTRAL BUSINESS DISTRICT Housed in a former bank, there's plenty of room to groove on the giant dance floor or saunter over to a seat in the old vault that sets the tone for the club's cool industrial vibe and flashy European style. *1100 Tulane Ave.* ☎ *504/587-3737. www.clubampersand.com. Cover $10–15. Map p 114.*

The Circle Bar UPTOWN This old pink and white house is dwarfed by commercial buildings on either side, which adds to the feeling of just hanging out at a friend's place with 40 easygoing buddies. Intimate performances by singer-songwriters add to the coziness. *1032 St. Charles Ave. at Lee Circle.* ☎ *504/588-2616. No cover. Map p 112.*

d.b.a. FAUBOURG MARIGNY The New Orleans version of the popular NYC original feels spacious and homey with a dark wood interior and dim lighting. Beer lovers should check out the long list of premium brews including Belgian draft beer and hand-drawn ales. *618 Frenchmen St.* ☎ *504/942-3731. www.drinkgoodstuff.com. Cover $5–$10. Map p 114.*

★ **The Dungeon** FRENCH QUARTER I stupidly went here during Mardi Gras and was nearly crushed, which made it really feel like a claustrophobic dungeon. Dark and scary in a B-movie kind of way, it's a good choice for a late, late night (doesn't open till midnight). *738 Toulouse St.* ☎ *504/523-5530. Cover $5. Map p 111.*

El Matador FRENCH QUARTER Shoot some pool or preen at the main circular bar and you just might see a celebrity or two nestled into a private, plush booth. *504 Esplanade Ave.* ☎ *504/586-0790. Cover $5–$15. Map p 111.*

★ **F&M Patio Bar** UPTOWN Sure, the worn-down camelback house with some crazy additions on the back ain't much to look at, but inside everyone from coeds to working professionals are playing pool, swaying to classic rock, or crowding into the vintage photo booth so they can show off their black-and-white pics on the walls. *4841 Tchoupitoulas St.* ☎ *504/895-6784. No cover. Map p 112.*

★ **One Eyed Jacks** FRENCH QUARTER With a cool, cozy theater feel this spot hosts everything from cabaret to comedy, plus Fast Times '80s Night (every Thurs), and old-fashioned burlesque that's miles away from the raunchiness of Bourbon Street. *615 Toulouse St.* ☎ *504/565-5400. www.oneeyedjacks.net. Cover $5–$10. Map p 111.*

★★ **The Sazerac Bar** FRENCH QUARTER After a couple years of rehab, the fab and posh Sazerac Bar, located in the newly refurbished Roosevelt (formerly the Fairmont), returns with its signature namesake cocktail and Ramos Gin Fizz, luxurious surroundings, and original 1930s Art Deco murals by artist Paul Ninas. *In the Roosevelt*

The bowling lanes at Mid-City Lanes Rock 'n' Bowl.

Hotel, 123 Baronne St. ☎ 504/529-4733. No cover. Map p 111.

Historic Bars

Lafitte's Blacksmith Shop
FRENCH QUARTER   You've found your perfect hangout if you like holing up in a dank, dark den among gregarious young locals. *941 Bourbon St.* ☎ *504/522-9377. No cover. Map p 111.*

★★ Napoleon House FRENCH QUARTER   Stop in for the signature Pimm's Cup at this historic place with low-key lighting, strong drinks, and a relaxing atmosphere. *500 Chartres St.* ☎ *504/524-9752. www.napoleonhouse.com. No cover. Map p 111.*

The Old Absinthe House
FRENCH QUARTER   Try the house specialty, the Absinthe House Frappe, which dates back to 1874. It still packs a punch even though the absinthe is now replaced with Herbsaint. *240 Bourbon St.* ☎ *504/523-3181. www.oldabsinthehouse.com. No cover. Map p 111.*

Old Absinthe House.

Jazz Clubs (Contemporary)
Donna's Bar & Grill FRENCH QUARTER   Donna's live and loud brass band music (think marching jazz band) gets people off of their feet and often into the street for an impromptu second-line parade. Take a cab home after dark. *800 N. Rampart St.* ☎ *504/596-6914. Cover $3–$10. Map p 111.*

Jazz Parlor FRENCH QUARTER   Though some Bourbon Street bars get away with a great location and don't offer much else, here you'll find authentic modern jazz, reasonably priced drinks, and good food (it helps to be owned by the famous Brennan restaurateur family). *125 Bourbon St.* ☎ *504/410-1000. No cover. One-drink minimum per set. Map p 111.*

★★ Snug Harbor FAUBOURG MARIGNY   I've started many evenings enjoying the modern jazz interpretations of homegrown chanteuse Charmaine Neville (niece to Aaron) and you'd be wise to do the same. *626 Frenchmen St.* ☎ *504/949-0696. www.snugjazz. com. Cover $10–$20. Map p 114.*

Sweet Lorraine's BYWATER This jazz establishment harkens back to another time when America's original music was the hottest sound around. A taxi is a must there and back. *1931 St. Claude Ave.* ☎ *504/945-9654. www.sweet lorrainesjazzclub.com. Cover $5–$15. Map p 114.*

Jazz Clubs (Traditional)
Fritzel's European Jazz Club
FRENCH QUARTER   After a night of entertaining, jazz musicians gather here in the wee hours to jam and let off some steam. *733 Bourbon St.* ☎ *504/561-0432. www.fritzelsjazz. net. No cover. One-drink minimum per set. Map p 111.*

Live music at Donna's Bar & Grill.

Maison Bourbon FRENCH QUARTER Dixieland jazz attracts an older set of folks who are happy just tapping their toes to the oldies but goodies. *641 Bourbon St. ☎ 504/522-8818. No cover. One-drink minimum. Map p 111.*

The Palm Court Jazz Café FRENCH QUARTER During hot weather you might want to make reservations because listening to old-fashioned jazz in air-conditioned comfort is priceless. Stick with drinks and pass on the expensive food. *1204 Decatur St. ☎ 504/525-0200. www.palmcourtjazz.com. No cover at bar; $8 at table. Map p 111.*

★★ Preservation Hall FRENCH QUARTER This no-frills establishment is run by a nonprofit group dedicated to the preservation of jazz. *726 St. Peter St. ☎ 800/785-5772 or ☎ 504/522-2841. www.preservationhall.com. Cover $10. Map p 111.*

Karaoke
★ Cat's Meow FRENCH QUARTER If you have the urge to make a fool of yourself or watch others take a crack at hit songs ("Dream On," anyone?), you won't find a place better. *701 Bourbon St. ☎ 504/523-1157.* *www.catsmeow-neworleans.com. Cover $5 under 21; no cover 21 and over. Map p 111.*

Piano Bars
★★★ The Bombay Club FRENCH QUARTER With a martini in hand—preferably the Breathless, made with SKYY vodka, white crème de cacao, and a splash of Godiva liqueur in a chocolate-rimmed glass—lounge in the luxurious, elegant atmosphere. *In the Prince Conti Hotel, 830 Conti St. ☎ 504/586-0972. www.thebombayclub.com. No cover. Map p 111.*

★★ Carousel Bar & Lounge FRENCH QUARTER The slowly revolving bar is a whimsical detail in one of the city's more storied and immaculate historic hotels. *In the Hotel Monteleone, 214 Royal St. ☎ 504/523-3341. www.hotelmonteleone.com. No cover. Map p 111.*

Feelings Café FAUBOURG MARIGNY Romantic yearnings are best expressed among the tropical plants and exposed brick of the intimate courtyard. Or you can sing to your beloved with backing by the piano player and the usual friendly folks. *2600 Chartres St. ☎ 504/945-2222.*

Pat O'Brien's.

www.feelingscafe.com. No cover.
Map p 114.

Pat O'Brien's FRENCH QUAR-
TER   I'll admit it, the bar's world-
famous Hurricane, a gigantic rum
drink served in a hurricane lamp–
style glass, is hard to resist, along
with the flaming fountain and spacious courtyard. That said, you'll
find nary a native. *718 St. Peter St.*
☎ *504/525-4823. www.patobriens.
com. No cover. Map p 111.*

Pubs

Carrollton Station CARROLL-
TON   A true (and tiny) neighborhood joint where old friends often
meet and new folks are made to feel
welcome. *8140 Willow St.* ☎ *504/
865-9190. Cover $5–$10. Map p 115.*

Cooter Brown's Tavern CAR-
ROLLTON   Greasy cheese fries pair
well with an astounding variety of
domestic and international beers.
509 S. Carrollton Ave. ☎ *504/866-
9104. No cover. Map p 115.*

Kerry Irish Pub FRENCH QUAR-
TER   Enjoy a pint of Guinness while
playing darts or pool or just sit
back and listen to live Irish or alternative folk music. *331 Decatur St.*
☎ *504/527-5954. No cover.
Map p 111.*

Rock/Alternative Venues

Checkpoint Charlie's FRENCH
QUARTER   Rock out to up-and-
coming bands in a typically smoky,
dark dive with an atypical crowd.
501 Esplanade Ave. ☎ *504/947-
0979. No cover. Map p 111.*

★★ The Howlin' Wolf WARE-
HOUSE DISTRICT   A hand-carved
mahogany bar (it once belonged to
Al Capone) and magnificent Micha-
lopoulos mural set the stage for
mainstream acts like (native son)
Harry Connick, Jr., Alison Krauss,
Jimmy Page, and the Barenaked
Ladies. *907 S. Peters St.* ☎ *504/522-
9653. www.howlin-wolf.com. Cover
$5–$20. Map p 113.* ●

The Best **Arts & Entertainment**

Arts & Entertainment Best Bets

Movie night at The Prytania Theatre.

Best **Costumes**
Delta Festival Ballet, Dixon Hall, Tulane University, *1010 Common St. (p 128)*

Best **High Note**
★★ New Orleans Opera Association, Mahalia Jackson Theatre, *1010 Common St. (p 128)*

Best **Gory Special Effects**
★ La Nuit Comedy Theater, *2301 Soniat St. (p 128)*

Best **Belly Laughs**
★ The National Comedy Company, Yo Mama's Bar & Grill, *727 St. Peter St. (p 129)*

Best **Place to Feel Your Stomach Drop**
Entergy IMAX Theatre, *1 Canal St. (p 129)*

Best **Nostalgic Night at the Movies**
★★★ The Prytania Theatre, *5339 Prytania St. (p 129)*

Best **Chance to Win Big**
★★ The Fair Grounds Race Course, *1751 Gentilly Blvd. (p 129)*

Best **Slam Dunk**
New Orleans Arena, *1501 Girod St. (p 130)*

Best **Stadium Crowd**
Louisiana Superdome, *1500 Poydras St. (p 130)*

Best **Preshow Cocktail**
★★ le chat noir, *715 St. Charles Ave. (p 131)*

Best **Use of a Stage**
★★★ Le Petit Theatre, *616 St. Peter St. (p 131)*

Best **Culture Shock**
Zeitgeist Multi-Disciplinary Arts Center, *1724 Oretha Castle Haley Blvd. (p 132)*

Previous page: A performance on-stage at the Mahalia Jackson Theatre.

French Quarter A & E

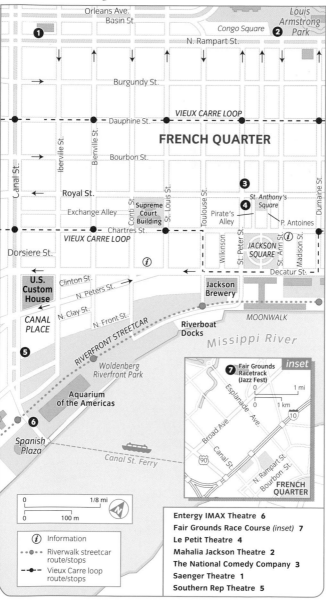

Entergy IMAX Theatre 6
Fair Grounds Race Course *(inset)* **7**
Le Petit Theatre 4
Mahalia Jackson Theatre 2
The National Comedy Company 3
Saenger Theatre 1
Southern Rep Theatre 5

Central Business District A & E

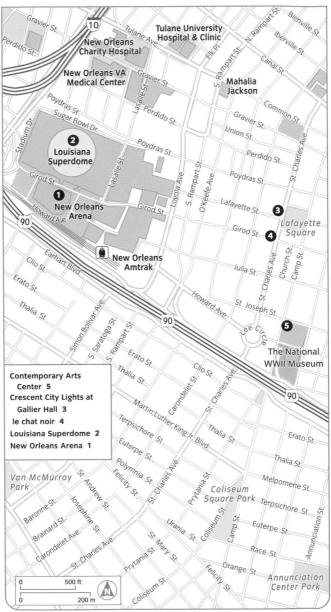

Gravier St.

Perdido St.

10

Tulane Ave.

New Orleans
Charity Hospital

New Orleans VA
Medical Center

Tulane University
Hospital & Clinic

N. Rampart St.

Bienville St.

Iberville St.

Elk Pl.

S. Rampart St.

Canal St.

Gravier St.

Mahalia
Jackson

Common St.

Stadium Dr.

Poydras St.

Sugar Bowl Dr.

LaSalle St.

Perdido St.

Gravier St.

Union St.

St. Charles Ave.

2
Louisiana
Superdome

Poydras St.

Poydras St.

Perdido St.

LaSalle St.

Loyola Ave.

Poydras St.

Girod St.

S. Rampart St.

O'Keefe Ave.

Lafayette St.

3

1
New Orleans
Arena

Howard Ave.

Girod St.

Girod St.

4

Lafayette
Square

90

St. Charles Ave.

Church St.

Camp St.

New Orleans
Amtrak

Julia St.

Earhart Blvd.

Clio St.

Erato St.

Thalia St.

Howard Ave.

St. Joseph St.

5

Simon Bolivar Ave.

S. Saratoga St.

S. Rampart St.

Erato St.

90

Clio St.

Lee Circle

The National
WWII Museum

Thalia St.

Carondelet St.

St. Charles Ave.

90

Erato St.

Thalia St.

Martin Luther King Jr Blvd

Thalia St.

Terpsichore St.

Euterpe St.

Polymnia St.

Prytania St.

Melpomene St.

Terpsichore St.

**Contemporary Arts
Center 5
Crescent City Lights at
Gallier Hall 3
le chat noir 4
Louisiana Superdome 2
New Orleans Arena 1**

Van McMurray
Park

St. Andrew St.

Felicity St.

St. Charles Ave.

Coliseum
Square Park

Euterpe St.

Annunciation St.

Baronne St.

Josephine St.

Brainard St.

Carondelet Ave.

St. Charles Ave.

Urania St.

St. Mary St.

Coliseum St.

Camp St.

Race St.

Prytania St.

Felicity St.

Orange St.

Annunciation
Center Park

Coliseum St.

0   500 ft

0   200 m

N

Uptown A & E

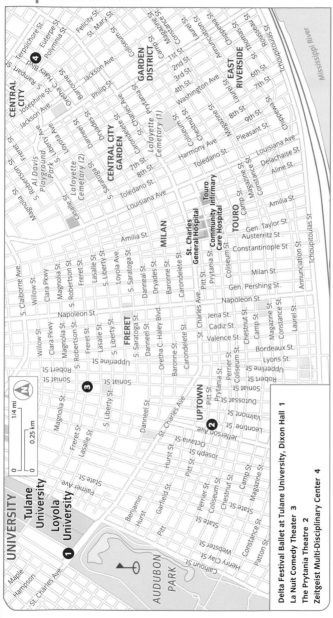

Delta Festival Ballet at Tulane University, Dixon Hall 1
La Nuit Comedy Theater 3
The Prytania Theatre 2
Zeitgeist Multi-Disciplinary Center 4

Arts & Entertainment A to Z

Classical Music, Opera & Dance

kids Delta Festival Ballet

UPTOWN   The city's oldest professional ballet company showcases local talent. Its annual holiday production of *The Nutcracker* with the Louisiana Philharmonic Orchestra is hugely popular, especially with families. *Tulane University, Dixon Halll, plus other locations around the city.* ☎ *504/836-7166. www.deltafestival ballet.com. Tickets $12–$50. Map p 127.*

Louisiana Philharmonic Orchestra

CENTRAL BUSINESS DISTRICT   Founded in 1991, the LPO is the only symphony in the nation whose musicians own and manage it. The season runs from September through May. *Mahalia Jackson Theatre, 1010 Common St., plus other locations around the city.* ☎ *504/523-6530. www.lpomusic. com. Tickets $15–$65. Map p 125.*

New Orleans Ballet Association

CENTRAL BUSINESS DISTRICT   Entertaining and educating Southern dance aficionados since 1969, NOBA hosts dance troupes from around the world in lieu of having its own company. The season runs from September through June. *Mahalia Jackson Theatre, 1010 Common St.* ☎ *504/522-0996. www. nobadance.com. Tickets $10–$70. Map p 112.*

★★ New Orleans Opera Association

CENTRAL BUSINESS DISTRICT   For more than 65 years, NOOA has presented classical opera pieces and more contemporary fare to appeal to younger audiences. *Mahalia Jackson Theatre, 1010 Common St.* ☎ *800/881-4459 or 504/529-2278. www.neworleansopera.org. Tickets $30–$125. Map p 125.*

Comedy

★ La Nuit Comedy Theater

UPTOWN   New Orleans is renowned for its cast of eccentric characters, so it was just a matter of time before a smart, sassy improv company put down roots. Lead by veteran comedian-actress Yvonne Landry, La Nuit also plays host to the week-long New Orleans Comedy

Outside the Mahalia Jackson Theatre.

The Entery IMAX Theatre is a great place to take the kids.

Arts Festival every February. If you have a morbid sense of humor, wear your old clothes to cult favorite Splatterhouse Theater, 2009 Ambie Award Winner for "Best Special Effects." *2301 Soniat St.* ☎ *504/899-0336. www.nolacomedy. com. Tickets $10. Map p 127.*

★ **The National Comedy Company** FRENCH QUARTER If you like *Whose Line Is It Anyway?* you'll love this Southern twist on the original. The audience calls the shots and the comics—some of whom have performed with Ben Stein, Ryan Stiles, and David Cross—surprise you with their wacky spontaneity. You'll laugh so hard you'll cry. *Yo Mama's Bar & Grill, 727 St. Peter St.* ☎ *504/523-7469. www.national comedycompany.com. Tickets $8–$10. Map p 125.*

Film

kids Entergy IMAX Theatre FRENCH QUARTER Make the steep climb to your seat and prepare to feel like you're actually in the movie. (Seriously, I once got motion sickness watching a documentary on flying.) Three-D films presented on the giant screen have featured everything from dinosaurs to contemporary action films such as The Dark Knight. *1 Canal St.* ☎ *800/774-7394 or 504/581-4629.*

www.auduboninstitute.org. Tickets $5–$8. Map p 125.

★★★ **The Prytania Theatre** UPTOWN This single-screen cinema is the last of its kind and the city's oldest operating theater, and yet it just went completely digital, so you get the best of both worlds. Octogenarian owner René Brunet will personally greet you at the door. I used to live right around the corner so we were regular patrons, and I can still sing the '50s era "Let's All Go to the Lobby" clip that precedes every film. Probably the strangest thing is asking for a ticket without having to say which show. Film choices run the gamut, from classics to the latest blockbusters. *5339 Prytania St.* ☎ *504/891-2787. www.theprytania.com. Tickets $5.25–$7.25. Map p 127.*

Sports Venues

★★ **The Fair Grounds Race Course** MID-CITY The nation's third-oldest horse-racing track has tenaciously overcome fire, hurricanes, world wars, and the Depression. The track and slots attract die-hard gamblers, moneyed socialites, and hooky-playing coeds. The air-conditioned modern clubhouse is fine, but my money is always on the grandstand, where I can feel the warm sun and see the horses kick

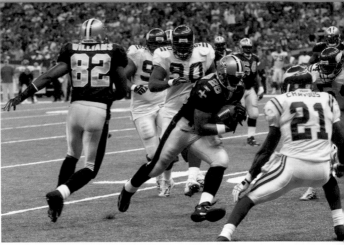

The New Orleans Saints play at the Louisiana Superdome.

up dust as they charge past. *1751 Gentilly Blvd.* ☎ *504/944-5515. www.fairgroundsracecourse.com. Tickets $6 clubhouse, free grandstand. Map p 129.*

Louisiana Superdome CENTRAL BUSINESS DISTRICT Oh, when the Saints, go marchin' in, you will hear the crowd scream with excitement. No matter their record, the New Orleans Saints have the best football fans around. The Superdome, their home, can hold 76,000 Saints fans or more than 100,000 concertgoers. Trade shows, conventions, and the annual Sugar Bowl also set up shop here. *1500 Poydras St.* ☎ *504/587-3663. www.superdome.com. Saints tickets $55–$329. Map p 126.*

New Orleans Arena CENTRAL BUSINESS DISTRICT The New Orleans Hornets basketball team continues to impress, due in no small part to All-Star point guard Chris Paul. The team's young top scorer is a fan favorite and brings out the best in his teammates. *1501 Girod St.* ☎ *504/525-HOOP. www. nba.com/hornets. Tickets $8–$1,700. Map p 126.*

New Orleans Zephyrs Field JEFFERSON Die-hard baseball fans root for the Zephyrs—the AAA farm team of the Houston Astros—in their spacious suburban stadium. They generally do well enough to help us forget yet another disappointing Saints season. *6000 Airline Dr., Jefferson.* ☎ *504/734-5155. www.zephyrsbaseball.com. Tickets $6–$15. Not mapped.*

Theaters

★ **Contemporary Arts Center** CENTRAL BUSINESS DISTRICT This social hub attracts fans of modern art, experimental plays, dance productions, concerts, and the occasional comedy and film screening. The rooms are small enough that every seat is a good one, although it can be a bit cramped when full. After the show, unwind with some coffee or wine at the Cyber Bar & Café. *900 Camp St.* ☎ *504/528-3800. www.cacno.org. Ticket prices vary. Map p 126.*

kids Crescent City Lights CEN-
TRAL BUSINESS DISTRICT Sup-
ported by the New Orleans
Recreation Department, CCL gives
local children a chance to strut their
stuff on stage. The summer production is usually kid-oriented, while the
fall one is a better bet for adults.
Musicals are the usual fare and
there's no dress code, so it's popular with families. *Gallier Hall, 705
Lafayette St.* ☎ *504/565-7860.
www.crescentcitylights.com. Tickets
$15. Map p 126.*

★★ **le chat noir** CENTRAL BUSI-
NESS DISTRICT Get dressed up
and come early for a cocktail at the
bar and stay for an experimental
play, cabaret, or live music. *715 St.
Charles Ave.* ☎ *504/581-5812.
www.cabaretlechatnoir.com. Tickets
$15–$34. Map p 126.*

★★★ **Le Petit Theatre du
Vieux Carre** FRENCH QUARTER
Le Petit Theatre is one of the oldest
nonprofessional theater troupes in
the United States. The company
presents everything from classic
and contemporary plays and musicals to experimental fare from local
writers. *616 St. Peter St.* ☎ *504/522-
2081. www.lepetittheatre.com. Tickets $35. Map p 125.*

Contemporary Arts Center.

Saenger Theatre FRENCH QUAR-
TER Opened in 1927 at a cost of
$2.5 million, the venerable Saenger
is listed on the National Register of
Historic Places. The interior resembles an Italian courtyard complete
with a "starry" sky thanks to 150
small lights formed into constella-
tions. Due to significant damage
from Katrina the theater remains
closed with plans to reopen by 2011.
143 N. Rampart St. ☎ *504/525-1052.
www.saengeramusements.com.
Map p 125.*

The New Orleans Arena is the home court of the NBA's New Orleans Hornets.

The "Stella" yelling contest at Le Petit Theatre at the annual Tennessee Williams festival.

Southern Rep Theatre FRENCH QUARTER   New Southern plays are showcased in this plain but comfortable theater in a multistoried, high-end shopping center. Casts include a mix of young green actors and experienced local talent. *The Shops at Canal Place.* ☎ *504/522-6545. www.southernrep.com. Tickets $18–$23. Map p 125.*

Zeitgeist Multi-Disciplinary Arts Center UPTOWN   Come here with an open mind; this is not your grandma's theater! The people-watching is just as fascinating as the experimental shows. For safety's sake, please take a cab. *1724 Oretha Castle Haley Blvd.* ☎ *504/ 525-2767. www.zeitgeistinc.net. Tickets $5–$7. Map p 127.* ●

9 The Best **Lodging**

Lodging Best Bets

Most **Luxurious**
★★★ Ritz-Carlton $$$ *921 Canal St. (p 145)*

Best **Views**
★ Omni Royal Orleans $$
621 St. Louis St. (p 144)

Most **Exclusive Hotel**
★★★ Le Pavillon Hotel $ *833 Poydras St. (p 143)*

Most **Historic**
★★★ Hotel Monteleone $$
214 Royal St. (p 142)

Hippest Hotel
★ W French Quarter $$$ *316 Chartres St. (p 146)*

Best **French Quarter Hotel**
★ Bourbon Orleans Hotel $$
717 Orleans St. (p 139)

Best **Moderately Priced Hotel**
★ Bienville House $$–$$$
320 Decatur St. (p 139)

Best **Bathrooms**
★★ McKendrick-Breaux House $$,
1474 Magazine St. (p 143)

Best **Family Hotel**
★ Holiday Inn–Chateau LeMoyne $$, *301 Dauphine St. (p 141)*

Best **Cheap Bed**
★★ St. Vincent's Guest House $
1507 Magazine St. (p 146)

Most **Romantic**
★★ Soniat House $$, *1133 Chartres St. (p 146)*

Best **Boutique Hotel**
★★★ International House $$
221 Camp St. (p 142)

Best **Hidden Gem**
★★ House on Bayou Road $$
2275 Bayou Rd. (p 142)

Best **Bed & Breakfast**
★ Grand Victorian Bed & Breakfast $$ *2727 St. Charles Ave. (p 141)*

A luxurious room at the Ritz-Carlton.

Previous page: The lobby of the Hotel Monteleone.

Uptown/Mid-City Lodging

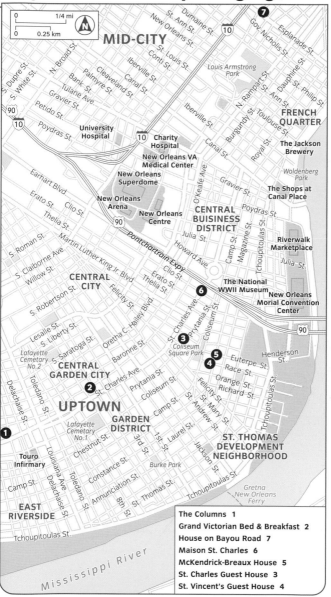

0	1/4 mi
0	0.25 km

MID-CITY

Louis Armstrong Park

FRENCH QUARTER

University Hospital

Charity Hospital

The Jackson Brewery

New Orleans VA Medical Center

New Orleans Superdome

Woldenberg Park

The Shops at Canal Place

New Orleans Arena

New Orleans Centre

CENTRAL BUISINESS DISTRICT

Riverwalk Marketplace

CENTRAL CITY

The National WWII Museum

New Orleans Morial Convention Center

Lafayette Cemetery No.2

CENTRAL GARDEN CITY

Coliseum Square Park

UPTOWN

Lafayette Cemetery No.1

GARDEN DISTRICT

ST. THOMAS DEVELOPMENT NEIGHBORHOOD

Touro Infirmary

Burke Park

Gretna New Orleans Ferry

EAST RIVERSIDE

Mississippi River

The Columns **1**
Grand Victorian Bed & Breakfast **2**
House on Bayou Road **7**
Maison St. Charles **6**
McKendrick-Breaux House **5**
St. Charles Guest House **3**
St. Vincent's Guest House **4**

French Quarter & Faubourg

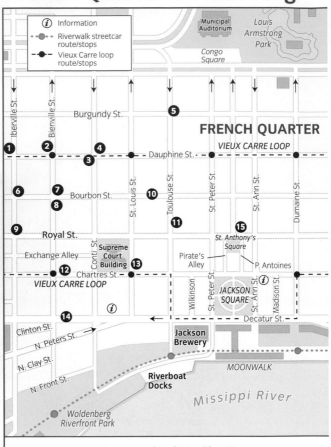

B&W Courtyards Bed & Breakfast **25**
Bienville House **14**
Bourbon Orleans Hotel **15**
Chateau Bourbon – Wyndham Historic Hotel **6**
Chateau Hotel **18**
Dauphine Orleans Hotel **4**
Frenchman **24**
Holiday Inn-Chateau LeMoyne **2**
Hotel Maison de Ville **11**
Hotel Monteleone **9**
Hotel Provincial **19**
Lafitte Guest House **17**
Lamothe House **22**

Marigny Lodging

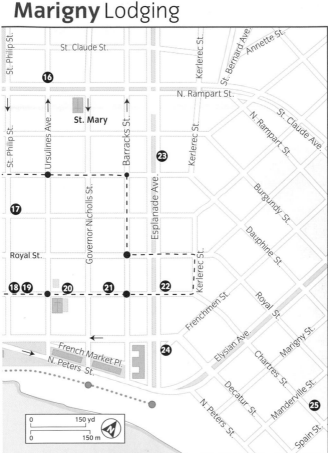

Le Richelieu Hotel **21**
Maison Dupuy **5**
Melrose Mansion **23**
New Orleans Guest House **16**
Omni Royal Orleans **13**
Prince Conti Hotel **3**
Ramada Plaza The Inn on Bourbon Street **10**
Ritz-Carlton New Orleans **1**
Royal Sonesta **7**
The Saint Louis **8**
Soniat House **20**
W French Quarter **12**

Central Business District Lodging

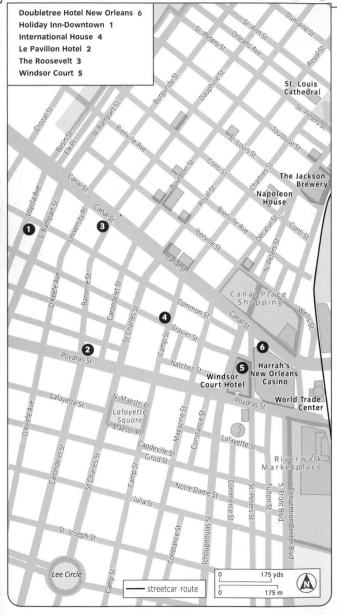

Doubletree Hotel New Orleans 6
Holiday Inn-Downtown 1
International House 4
Le Pavillon Hotel 2
The Roosevelt 3
Windsor Court 5

St. Ann St.
Dumaine St.
Orleans Ave.
St. Peters St.
Royal St.
St. Louis Cathedral
St. Peters St.
Crozat St.
Basin St.
Elk Pl.
N. Rampart St.
Burgundy St.
Dauphine St.
Toulouse St.
Bienville Ave.
St. Louis St.
Conti St.
The Jackson Brewery
Canal St.
Bourbon St.
Royal St.
Napoleon House
Loyola Ave.
S. Rampart St.
University Pl.
Canal St.
Bienville Ave.
Chartres St.
Decatur St.
Conti St.
Iberville St.
Canal St.
N. Peters St.
O'Keefe Ave.
Baronne St.
Carondelet St.
St. Charles St.
Canal Place Shopping
Common St.
Canal St.
Wells St.
Camp St.
Gravier St.
Poydras St.
Natchez St.
Windsor Court Hotel
Harrah's New Orleans Casino
World Trade Center
Lafayette St.
N. Maestri Pl.
Lafayette Square
S. Maestri Pl.
Magazine St.
Constance St.
Poydras St.
O'Keefe Ave.
Carondelet St.
St. Charles St.
Camp St.
Capdeville St.
Girod St.
Lafayette St.
Riverwalk Marketplace
Notre Dame St.
Commerce St.
St. Peters St.
Fulton St.
S. Front Blvd.
Convention Center Blvd.
Julia St.
Tchoupitoulas St.
Constance St.
St. Joseph St.
Lee Circle
Camp St.

— streetcar route

0   175 yds
0   175 m

Lodging A to Z

B&W Courtyards Bed & Breakfast FAUBOURG MARIGNY   Most of the uniquely decorated guest rooms open onto a quiet courtyard. Your best bet is the former slave quarters converted into a private tropical retreat. *2425 Chartres St.* ☎ *800/585-5731 or 504/945-9418. www.bandwcourtyards.com. 6 units. Doubles $99–$250. AE, DISC, MC, V. Map p 137.*

★ **Bienville House** FRENCH QUARTER   The classically elegant interior features hand-painted wall murals. Some rooms have a wrought-iron balcony with a view of the flagstone courtyard. There's also a saltwater pool. *320 Decatur St.* ☎ *800/535-7836 or 504/529-2345. www.bienville house.com. 18 units. Doubles $89–$650. AE, DC, DISC, MC, V. Map p 137.*

A sitting area at Bienville House.

★ **kids Bourbon Orleans Hotel** FRENCH QUARTER   This lavish hotel has got it all: location, history, and good service. Rooms on the Royal Street side are less noisy. Kids will enjoy the outdoor pool and can sleep on pullout sofas in the bilevel suites. *717 Orleans St.* ☎ *504/523-2222. www.bourbonorleans.com. 40 units. Doubles $139–$329. AE, DC, DISC, MC, V. Map p 137.*

The elegant lobby at Bourbon Orleans Hotel.

A room at the Chateau Bourbon.

Chateau Bourbon–Wyndham Historic Hotel
FRENCH QUARTER Located in the late-19th-century D. H. Holmes Department Store building, the Chateau Bourbon's rooms (large, though nonspecific in style or charm) benefited from a post-Katrina makeover. A statue of Ignatius Reilly, the hero of Pulitzer Prize–winning novel *A Confederacy of Dunces,* greets visitors at the hotel's Canal Street entrance. *800 Iberville St.* ☎ *877/999-3223 or 504/586-0800. www.wyndham.com. 251 units. Doubles $99–$350. AE, DC, DISC, MC, V. Map p 137.*

Chateau Hotel
FRENCH QUARTER A good deal and a good location, the Chateau offers European charm and some peace and quiet just a stone's throw from busy Bourbon Street. Clean rooms have antique furnishings. *1001 Chartres St.* ☎ *504/524-9636. www.chateau hotel.com. 45 units. Doubles $89–$159. AE, DC, MC, V. Map p 137.*

★★ The Columns
UPTOWN The rooms are cozy and the dining area is worn in a well-loved way, but the real draw is sipping drinks on the huge, shady porch while listening to locals gossip and the streetcar rattle by. You may recognize this site as the setting for Louis Malle's film about Storyville, *Pretty Baby. 3811 St. Charles Ave.* ☎ *800/445-9308 or 504/899-9308. www.thecolumns. com. 22 units. Doubles $160–$230. AE, MC, V. Map p 135.*

kids Dauphine Orleans Hotel
FRENCH QUARTER Stay here for the perfect combo of vintage charm and modern perks. The multiple lovely private courtyards are also a draw. John James Audubon used the rear of the building as a studio. *415 Dauphine St.* ☎ *800/521-7111 or 504/586-1800. www.dauphine orleans.com. 111 units. Doubles $149–$269. AE, DC, DISC, MC, V. Map p 137.*

kids Doubletree Hotel New Orleans
CENTRAL BUSINESS DISTRICT Expect the usual from this clean, comfortable chain hotel.

The Columns.

Grand Victorian Bed & Breakfast.

Decent size rooms and a laid-back atmosphere are a plus for families. At check-in, the kids get chocolate-chip cookies, plus who wouldn't love a rooftop pool? *300 Canal St.* ☎ *888/874-9074 or 504/581-1300. www.doubletree.com. 550 units. Doubles $79–$229. AE, DC, DISC, MC, V. Map p 138.*

Frenchmen FAUBOURG MARIGNY Typical of the times, the rooms in these adjoining 1860s Creole town houses are teeny, but you'll probably spend most of your time in the pool or hot tub in the brick courtyard anyway. *417 Frenchmen St.* ☎ *800/831-1781 or 504/948-2166. www.frenchmenhotel.com. 12 units. Doubles $74–$299. AE, DISC, MC, V. Map p 137.*

★ **Grand Victorian Bed & Breakfast** UPTOWN This gorgeous 1893 historic home has been transformed into the grandest B&B on the avenue. Expect elegantly furnished rooms and some baths with Jacuzzi tubs. *2727 St. Charles Ave.* ☎ *800/977-0008 or 504/895-1104. www.gvbb.com. 8 units. Doubles $150–$350. AE, DISC, MC, V. Map p 135.*

★ **kids Holiday Inn–Chateau LeMoyne** FRENCH QUARTER Not bad for a chain, featuring comfortable albeit bland rooms and convenient walking distance to family-friendly attractions. *301 Dauphine St.* ☎ *800/747-3279 or 504/581-1303. www.sixcontinentshotels.com/ holiday-inn. 250 units. Doubles $159–$244. AE, DC, DISC, MC, V. Map p 137.*

Holiday Inn–Downtown CENTRAL BUSINESS DISTRICT You'll find clean, good-size rooms here, typical of the Holiday Inn chain. Sports fans like the proximity to the Superdome and New Orleans Arena for football and basketball, respectively. It's also a popular choice for Essence Fest. *330 Loyola Ave.* ☎ *800/535-7830 or 504/581-1600. www.holidayinndowntown superdome.com. 500 units. Doubles $94–$209. Children 18 and under free in parent's room. AE, DC, DISC, MC, V. Map p 138.*

Hotel Maison de Ville FRENCH QUARTER The Bourbon Street side of this atmospheric and romantic hotel (Tennessee Williams was a frequent guest) can be noisy, so be sure to inquire about room location when booking. To be assured a decent night's sleep, book one of the charming Audubon Cottages. Temporarily closed due to a fire

The rooftop pool at the Hotel Monteleone.

next door, the hotel should be reopened by the time you read this. *727 Toulouse St.* ☎ *800/634-1600 or 504/561-5858. www.maisondeville. com. 18 units. Doubles $199–$249. AE, DC, MC, V. Map p 137.*

★★★ Hotel Monteleone

FRENCH QUARTER   One dizzying look at the revolving Carousel Bar and the luxurious lobby and you'll know why literary lions like William Faulkner, Richard Ford, Ernest Hemingway, Rebecca Wells, Eudora Welty, and Tennessee Williams stayed here. A basic room can be small, so go for a two-room suite if you want to stretch out. Be sure to enjoy the rooftop pool. *214 Royal St.* ☎ *800/535-9595 or 504/523-3341. www.hotelmonteleone.com. 600 units. Doubles $199–$275. Children under 18 stay free in their parent's room. AE, DC, DISC, MC, V. Map p 137.*

Hotel Provincial FRENCH QUARTER   Run by the Dupepe family since 1969, you'd never guess that these luxurious surroundings—high ceilings and French and Creole antiques furnish the hotel—were once the site of a Civil War hospital. *1024 Chartres St.* ☎ *800/535-7922 or 504/581-4995. www.hotelprovincial.com. 55 units. Doubles $79–$289. AE, DC, DISC, MC, V. Map p 137.*

★★ House on Bayou Road

MID-CITY   Experience history and romance in this petite 18th-century Creole plantation. Southern cooking classes are often offered on-site. *2275 Bayou Rd.* ☎ *800/882-2968 or 504/945-0992. www.houseonbayou road.com. 8 units. Doubles $135–$320. AE, MC, V. Map p 135.*

★★★ International House

CENTRAL BUSINESS DISTRICT   This sensual, state-of-the-art sanctuary showcases the European, African, and Caribbean heritage of the city. A top of the line boutique hotel, the International House attracts media types and other travelers looking for a sophisticated, modern stay in this cultured, history-rich city. *221 Camp*

The House on Bayou Road is a comfortable and romantic guesthouse.

St. ☎ 800/633-5770 or 504/553-9550. www.ihhotel.com. 134 units. Doubles $149–$379. AE, DC, MC, V. Map p 138.

Lafitte Guest House FRENCH QUARTER   Built in 1849, the three-story brick mansion features wrought-iron balconies, Victorian flair, and pralines on the pillows. Guests are invited to socialize over wine and cheese in the parlor every afternoon. 1003 Bourbon St. ☎ 800/331-7971 or 504/581-2678. www.lafitteguesthouse.com. 14 units. Doubles $159–$229. AE, DC, DISC, MC, V. Map p 137.

Lamothe House FRENCH QUARTER   For the unfussy traveler who prefers a lived-in homey look where you can put your feet up on the coffee table. A courtyard with banana trees offers a quiet respite. 621 Esplanade Ave. ☎ 800/367-5858 or 504/947-1161. www.lamothehouse.com. 20 units. Doubles $74–$275. AE, DISC, MC, V. Map p 137.

★★★ Le Pavillon Hotel CENTRAL BUSINESS DISTRICT   Extravagance, thy name is Le Pavillon. The soaring lobby's crystal chandeliers, Oriental rugs, and rich oil paintings serve as the backdrop for signature peanut-butter-and-jelly sandwiches served on a silver platter with chocolates and milk nightly. This combination of whim and elegance is what makes Le Pavillon such a special place to stay. 833 Poydras St. ☎ 800/535-9095 or 504/581-3111. www.lepavillon.com. 300 units. Doubles $149–$179. AE, DC, DISC, MC, V. Map p 138.

kids Le Richelieu Hotel FRENCH QUARTER   Sir Paul McCartney and his late wife, Linda, stayed here with their kids back in the day when he was working on a Wings album. Despite the old-world charm and celebrity appeal, the convenient location and pool still make it a kid-friendly choice. 1234 Chartres St.

The sleek, sophisticated lobby of the International House.

☎ 800/535-9653 or 504/529-2492. www.lerichelieuhotel.com. 86 units. Doubles $95–$180. AE, DC, DISC, MC, V. Map p 137.

kids Maison Dupuy FRENCH QUARTER   This is a picturesque luxury hotel with impeccable service within walking distance of Bourbon Street, but far enough away to boast quiet rooms for a good night's sleep. If you want a balcony, be sure to ask if it's semiprivate first. This was once the site of the first cotton press in the United States. 1001 Toulouse St. ☎ 800/535-9177 or 504/586-8000. www.maisondupuy.com. 175 units. Doubles $99–$269. AE, DC, DISC, MC, V. Map p 137.

★ Maison St. Charles LOWER GARDEN DISTRICT   The inn is comprised of five large antebellum town homes and some newer construction, which makes for an eclectic mix of rooms, plus tropical courtyard and pool. For safety, stick close to the avenue. 1319 St. Charles Ave. ☎ 504/522-0187. www.maisonstcharles.com. 165 units. Doubles $89–$189. Map p 135.

★★ McKendrick-Breaux House LOWER GARDEN DISTRICT   This spacious Greek Revival mansion

A shady, sweet spot at the McKendrick-Breaux House.

located in a hip neighborhood with plenty of restaurants and shops within walking distance offers atmospheric antique-filled rooms with artwork by local artists. *1474 Magazine St.* ☎ *888/570-1700 or 504/586-1700. www.mckendrick-breaux.com. 9 units. Doubles $135–$235. AE, MC, V. Map p 135.*

Melrose Mansion FAUBOURG MARIGNY This meticulously restored historic home has tasteful Victorian decor (no flowery wallpaper here) in its well-maintained and spacious accommodations. *937 Esplanade Ave.* ☎ *800/650-3323 or 504/944-2255. www.melrosegroup.com. 15 units. Doubles $225–$275. AE, DISC, MC, V. Map p 137.*

Inside the Melrose Mansion.

★ **New Orleans Guest House**
FRENCH QUARTER Hard to miss, this bright pink gay-friendly inn offers generously sized rooms and helpful staff. It sits on the edge of the Quarter, so take a cab at night. *1118 Ursulines St.* ☎ *800/562-1177 or 504/566-1177. www.neworleans.com/nogh. 14 units. Doubles $79–$199. AE, MC, V. Map p 137.*

★ kids **Omni Royal Orleans**
FRENCH QUARTER An elegant member of the Omni chain, this location is popular with parents because of its inexpensive babysitting service and nearby museums and parks. Request a room with double beds or a rollaway bed for the kids. *621 St. Louis St.* ☎ *800-THE-OMNI [843-6664] or 504/529-5333. www.omniroyalorleans.com. 346 units. Doubles $169–$339. Children 18 and under free with parent. AE, DC, DISC, MC, V. Map p 137.*

Prince Conti Hotel FRENCH QUARTER This is a great choice if you're looking for a reasonably priced, clean room and don't mind the lack of upscale amenities such as a pool and courtyard. It's all good . . . well, except for the tiny bathrooms. Stop by the Bombay Club for the best martinis in town (see chapter 7). *830 Conti St.* ☎ *800/366-2743 or 504/529-4172. www.princecontihotel.com.*

The famous Sazerac Bar at the Roosevelt hotel.

73 units. Doubles $129–$199. AE, DC, DISC, MC, V. Map p 137.

Ramada Plaza–The Inn on Bourbon Street FRENCH QUARTER   Grab a room with a balcony for Mardi Gras mayhem. Any other time of the year, save your money and stay elsewhere. *541 Bourbon St.* ☎ *800/535-7891 or 504/524-7611. www.innonbourbon.com. 186 units. Doubles $219–$299. AE, DC, DISC, MC, V. Map p 137.*

★★★ Ritz-Carlton New Orleans FRENCH QUARTER   Louisiana's only AAA Five Diamond luxury hotel underwent an extravagant post-Katrina renovation that re-creates the ambience of a magnificent antebellum mansion but still offers modern amenities and service. A world-class spa and fine restaurant make it easy to self indulge. *921 Canal St.* ☎ *800/241-3333 or 504/524-1331. www.ritzcarlton.com. 300 units. Doubles $239–$329. AF, DISC, MC, V. Map p 137.*

★★★ kids The Roosevelt CENTRAL BUSINESS DISTRICT   The elegant and timeless hotel (formerly known as the Fairmont) where legendary politicians such as President Bill Clinton and Huey Long stayed offers upscale amenities such as the famous Sazerac Bar and Restaurant, and a rooftop pool, workout area, and beauty shop. A winter wonderland lobby display during the holidays entertains

children of all ages. *123 Baronne St.* ☎ *800/441-1414 or 504/529-7111. www.fairmont.com/neworleans. 500 units. Doubles $99–$299. Children under 18 free in parent's room. AE, DC, DISC, MC, V. Map p 138.*

Royal Sonesta FRENCH QUARTER   Bourbon Street action dressed up in a classy package. To achieve a good night's sleep, ask for an inside-facing room. *300 Bourbon St.* ☎ *800/SONESTA or 504/586-0300. www.royalsonestano.com. 325 units. Doubles $249–$389. AE, DC, DISC, MC, V. Map p 137.*

★ St. Charles Guest House LOWER GARDEN DISTRICT   This no-frills funky place appeals to college kids and adventure seekers who just need a place to catch some zzz's. The rooms don't have phones (and some have no air-conditioning), but there is a lovely little courtyard with a swimming pool. *1748 Prytania St.* ☎ *504/523-6556. www.stcharles guesthouse.com. 8 units. Doubles $50–$75. AE, MC, V. Map p 135.*

The Saint Louis FRENCH QUARTER   If you were disappointed to learn that the French Quarter reflects more of a Spanish influence, you can indulge your inner Francophile here among the Parisian-themed decor and its acclaimed Louis XVI restaurant. *730 Bienville St.* ☎ *800/535-9111 or 504/581-7300. www.stlouishotel.com. 97 units. Doubles $145–$335. Children under 12*

A charming sitting area at Soniat House.

free in parent's room. AE, DC, DISC, MC, V. Map p 137.

★★ St. Vincent's Guest House
LOWER GARDEN DISTRICT   The former early-20th-century brick orphanage has been transformed into an extraordinarily affordable place to stay (some hostel-style accommodations available). It doesn't skimp on atmosphere, service, or amenities. *1507 Magazine St.* ☎ *504/302-9606. www.stvguest house.com. 70 units. Hostel $25 per person, doubles $45–$89. AE, DC, DISC, MC, V. Map p 135.*

★★ Soniat House FRENCH QUAR-
TER   With an opulent, plantation-era atmosphere the Soniat House offers fine French and English antiques and Oriental rugs, but the bathrooms are small. See p. 29, **⑬**. *1133 Chartres St.* ☎ *800/544-8808 or 504/522-0570. www.soniathouse. com. 35 units. Doubles $240–$295. Children under 13 not permitted. AE, MC, V. Map p 137.*

★ W French Quarter FRENCH
QUARTER   This superchic, contemporary hotel attracts mostly young professionals. Locals eat up the Italian/Creole cuisine at in-house Bacco (see chapter 6). *316 Chartres St.* ☎ *800/448-4927 or 504/581-1200.*

www.whotels.com. 85 units. Doubles $425–$499. Children under 16 free in parent's room. AE, DC, DISC, MC, V. Map p 137.

★★★ Windsor Court CENTRAL
BUSINESS DISTRICT   You get what you pay for here—excellent service, large suites, and all the high-end amenities you could possibly want. *300 Gravier St.* ☎ *888/596-0955 or 504/523-6000. www.windsorcourt hotel.com. 300 units. Doubles $195–$450. Children under 12 free in parent's room. AE, DC, DISC, MC, V. Map p 138.* ●

High-end luxury at the Windsor Court hotel.

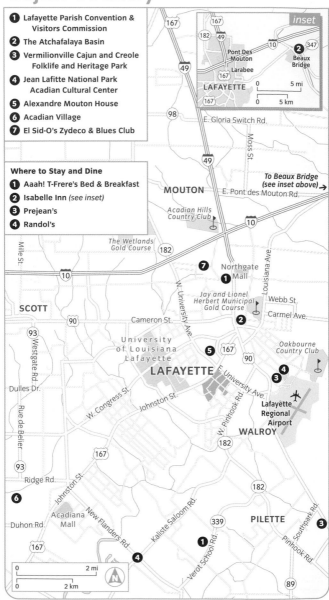

Cajun Country

1. Lafayette Parish Convention & Visitors Commission
2. The Atchafalaya Basin
3. Vermilionville Cajun and Creole Folklife and Heritage Park
4. Jean Lafitte National Park Acadian Cultural Center
5. Alexandre Mouton House
6. Acadian Village
7. El Sid-O's Zydeco & Blues Club

Where to Stay and Dine

1. Aaah! T-Frere's Bed & Breakfast
2. Isabelle Inn *(see inset)*
3. Prejean's
4. Randol's

inset

Pont Des Mouton

Larabee

Beaux Bridge

LAFAYETTE

0   5 mi

0   5 km

E. Gloria Switch Rd.

MOUTON

To Beaux Bridge (see inset above) →

E. Pont des Mouton Rd.

Acadian Hills Country Club

The Wetlands Gold Course

Northgate Mall

Jay and Lionel Herbert Municipal Gold Course

Webb St.

Carmel Ave.

SCOTT

Cameron St.

University of Louisiana Lafayette

Oakbourne Country Club

LAFAYETTE

E. University Ave.

Westgate Rd.

Dulles Dr.

W. Congress St.

Johnston St.

Lafayette Regional Airport

WALROY

Rue de Belier

Ridge Rd.

Acadiana Mall

New Flanders Rd.

PILETTE

Duhon Rd.

Kaliste Saloom Rd.

Verot School Rd.

Southpark Rd.

Pinhook Rd.

0   2 mi

0   2 km

Previous page: A group tours the Barataria Preserve outside Lafitte.

Cajuns have influenced Louisiana cooking, music, and language since their Acadian ancestors were deported from a colony in Nova Scotia more than 300 years ago. The French-speaking people found exile in southern Louisiana, which was under control of France at the time. They settled unwanted swampland, isolated but free to create their own way of life and culture. Despite modern pressures to conform, the Cajun community remains strong, particularly in Lafayette, just a few hours from New Orleans. START: Head west on Interstate 10 from New Orleans. Lafayette, your first stop, is approximately 135 miles (217km) 2½ hr. away.

❶ The Lafayette Parish Convention and Visitors Commission. This is the perfect place to stop and plan your day with the help of friendly staff, brochures, and maps. Feel free to ask about the city's combination of Cajun, Caribbean, French, and Spanish influences, making it one of the world's most unique cultures. *1400 NW Evangeline Thruway, Lafayette.* ☎ *800/346-1958 or 337/232-3737. www.lafayettetravel.com. Weekdays 8:30am–5pm, weekends 9am–5pm.*

Bird in Atchafalaya Basin swamp.

Head south on NW Evangeline Thruway, turn left at Dudley Avenue, then right at NW Evangeline Thruway/US-167. Turn left on Mudd Avenue/US-90 and turn right on N. Sterling Street (1 mile/ 1.6km, 3 min.).

❷ The Atchafalaya Basin. This is the largest river swamp in the United States and home to abundant fish, birds (some endangered), and other wildlife. Environmentally conscious father-son guides Coerte A. Voorhies, Jr., a semiretired geologist, and Kim B. Voorhies, an avid hunter/fisherman, are extremely knowledgeable about its delicate and varied ecosystems and southern Louisiana culture in general. *338 N. Sterling St., Lafayette.* ☎ *337/ 261-5150. www.theatchafalaya experience.com. Tours by appointment only. Call for fares (depends on length of boat ride and what you*

want to see). Departures twice daily (weather permitting).

Head south on N. Sterling Street then left on E. Simcoe Street. Turn right at Surrey Street then right again at Fisher Road (2 miles/3.2km, 7 min.).

❸ kids Vermilionville Cajun and Creole Folklife and Heritage Park. Perhaps a bit more Disneyfied with its costumed, dancing Cajuns, it's still a fun way to explore a unique American culture. *300 Fisher Rd., Lafayette.* ☎ *866/99-BAYOU or 337/233-4077. www.vermilionville.org. Admission $8 adults, $6.50 seniors, $5 children 6–14, free children 5 and under. Tues–Sun 10am–4pm.*

Go 2 blocks southeast on Fisher Road.

❹ kids Jean Lafitte National Park Acadian Cultural Center.

A display at Jean Lafitte National Park Acadian Cultural Center.

Learn how the Acadian people were exiled from Nova Scotia and settled in the swamps of southern Louisiana where their isolation lead to the creation of a unique way of life. *501 Fisher Rd., Lafayette.* ☎ *337/ 232-0789. www.nps.gov/Jela. Free admission; donations welcome. Daily 8am–5pm, movie 9am–4pm on the hour.*

Head east on Fisher Road then turn right on Surrey Street. Continue on E. University Avenue. Turn right at Lafayette Street.

5 Alexandre Mouton House. This elegant antebellum home on the National Register of Historic Places was originally built for Vermilionville founder Jean Mouton. It now houses the Lafayette Museum's collection of Acadian history and culture. *1122 Lafayette St., Lafayette.* ☎ *337/234-2208. Admission $3 adults, $2 seniors, $1 children. Tues–Sat 9am–4:30pm, Sun 1–4pm.*

Head south on Lafayette Street. Turn left at LA-182/W. University Avenue, then right at Johnston Street/US-167 and continue for 5½ miles (8.7km). Turn right at Duhon Road/LA-342, right at W. Broussard Road, right at New Hope Road, then left at Greenleaf Drive.

6 kids Acadian Village. This "folklife museum" depicts an authentic 19th-century Cajun bayou community. The cute gift shop sells handmade Cajun crafts and books. *200 Greenleaf Dr., Lafayette.* ☎ *800/962-9133 or 337/981-2364. www.acadianvillage.org. Admission $8 adults, $7 seniors, $5 children 6–14, free children 5 and under. Daily 10am–4pm.*

7 El Sid-O's Zydeco & Blues Club. This plain commercial building comes alive with funky zydeco music guaranteed to get you on the dance floor. Respected local zydeco and Cajun musicians are known to stop by and share the stage. *1523 Martin Luther King Dr., Lafayette.* ☎ *337/235-0647. Cover $7. Fri–Sat 9pm–2am, occasionally Sun–Mon during festival weekends.*

Where to Stay & Dine

Lodging
★★ Aaah! T-Frere's Bed & Breakfast.
If you have a sense of humor, you'll love the funny family that runs this comfortable inn. Former chef Maugie Pastor serves delicious full breakfasts with whimsical names like "Ooh La La, Mardi Gras" while dressed in bright red silk pajamas. All rooms boast private baths; my favorite is the Mary Room for its huge antique bed and more masculine counterpoint to the country Victorian elsewhere. *1905 Verot School Rd., Lafayette.* ☎ *800/984-9347 or 337/ 984-9347. www.tfreres.com. 8 units.*

At the Acadian Village.

Doubles $95-$120 w/breakfast. AE, DC, DISC, MC, V.

★ **kids** **Isabelle Inn.** Just 15 minutes outside Lafayette, staying in this spacious home is well worth the extra effort. The Richard Room is beautifully appointed with antiques and offers a gorgeous view from the balcony. I also like the serene cottage feel of the Allison Room. Unlike most B&Bs, kids are welcome and will love the pool and exploring the garden. *1130 Berard St., Breaux Bridge.* ☎ *337/412-0455. www. isabelleinn.com. 5 units. Doubles $165. AE, MC, V.*

Dining

★★★ **kids** **Prejean's.** All things Cajun greet you as soon as you step inside, including the photo-op-friendly 14-foot (4.2m) alligator Big Al posed in the middle of the swamp-themed dining room. Get all your favorites on one plate—its signature seafood platter features fried frog leg, shrimp, oysters, catfish, alligator, stuffed shrimp, and stuffed crab, and is served with spicy sides like dirty rice or corn *maque choux*. Live Cajun music nightly. *3480 NE Evangeline Thruway (I-49), Lafayette.* ☎ *337/896-3247. www.prejeans. com. Reservations recommended.*

Entrees $16–$28. AE, DC, DISC, MC, V. Breakfast, lunch & dinner daily.

Randol's. Owner Frank Randol fosters a community spirit here, reminiscent of a simpler time when people would gather to eat good, simple food and dance the night away. Indulge in the cheesy, gooey Louisiana crawfish enchiladas then work off those calories on the dance floor. Locals will show you all the right moves. *2320 Kaliste Saloom Rd., Lafayette.* ☎ *800/962-2586 or 337/981-7080. www.randols.com. Entrees $8–$28. MC, V. Dinner served Sun–Thurs 5–10pm, Fri–Sat 5–11pm.*

Randol's dance floor.

Lafitte

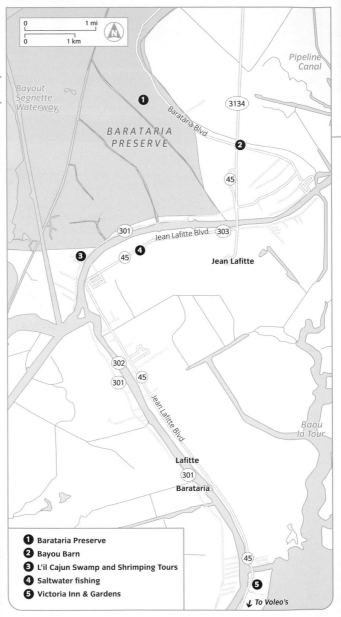

1. Barataria Preserve
2. Bayou Barn
3. L'il Cajun Swamp and Shrimping Tours
4. Saltwater fishing
5. Victoria Inn & Gardens

L afitte is an intriguing small town where many people still fish for a living and wealthy New Orleanians build sprawling country homes. When the cityscape seems too hurried and crowded, we escape here to the natural beauty and open water of our favorite shrimping village. Despite the threats of hurricane flooding and encroaching development, local tradition lives on. START: **From New Orleans, take Interstate 10 east heading toward the Mississippi River, cross the Crescent City Connection, and continue on what becomes the West Bank Expressway (yes, you're headed east, but it's the west side of the river bank), exit at 4B Barataria Boulevard, turn left at the second stoplight onto Barataria Boulevard, then left on Lafitte Parkway.**

❶ The Barataria Preserve.

This preserve offers hiking, fishing, and canoeing along freshwater marshlands and sleepy bayous. There are plenty of prime bird-watching opportunities. Remember mosquito repellent! *Visitor Center, 6488 Barataria Blvd., Marrero.* ☎ *504/589-2330. www.nps.gov/ jela/barataria-preserve.htm. Free admission, donations welcome. Trails open daily 7am–dusk, visitor center open daily 9am–5pm.*

Head southwest on Barataria Blvd/LA-301.

❷ Bayou Barn.

It's not unusual for a local establishment to be all things to all people. Bayou Barn is a rustic, open-air "restaurant" (think picnic tables under a roof) that packs in the crowds for its weekly Sunday Cajun dances. During the day, it rents out canoes for exploring beautiful Bayou des Familles. Just beware of the large alligator gar fish that rest below the surface. Take my word for it that you do not want to bop one on the head with your paddle! Rentals must be returned by dark. *7145 Barataria Blvd., Marrero.* ☎ *800/862-2968 or 504/689-2663. www.bayoubarn.com. Canoe rentals $20/hr. Mon–Fri 10am–5pm, Sat–Sun 10am–8pm.*

Head southwest on Barataria Blvd/LA-301. Located just outside Jean Lafitte National Park and next to Frank's Boat Launch.

❸ kids L'il Cajun Swamp and Shrimping Tours.

Captain Cyrus Blanchard is a larger-than-life personality who will show you why it's important to preserve the environment and the local way of life. Kids will get a kick out of his resident alligator, Julie. *Hwy. 301, just outside Jean Lafitte National Park, next to Frank's Boat Launch, Crowne Point.* ☎ *800/725-3213 or 504/689-3213. Admission $17 adults, $15 seniors, $13 children 4–12, and*

The lush Barataria Preserve.

Bayou Barn canoes.

free children 3 and under. Tours daily 10am and 2pm.

Head north on Barataria Blvd/ LA-301. Turn slightly right at LA-45, then left to continue on LA-45. Turn right at LA-3134/LA-45. Turn left at Jean Lafitte Blvd/ LA-303/LA-45. Destination will be on right.

❹ **Saltwater fishing.** Captain Phil Robichaux or a member of his professional fishing charter team can help you find where the redfish and speckled trout are lurking. The price includes all terminal tackle, artificial baits, gas, oil, ice, fish cleaning, and rods and reels.

The pleasant grounds of Victoria Inn & Gardens.

Customers must provide their own beverages, food, and fishing license. The latter are required by the State of Louisiana Department of Wildlife and Fisheries and are available for purchase online or by phone (www. wlf.state.la.us; ☎ 888/765-2602). Fishing permits cost $9.50 (annual) resident, $5 (1 day) or $15 (4 days) nonresident, plus service fee if ordered online/by phone. *1842 Jean Lafitte Blvd., Lafitte. ☎ 504/689-2006. www.rodnreel.com/captphil. Departures daily 6–6:30am, return 1:30–2:30pm.*

Head southwest on Jean Lafitte Blvd/LA-45.

❺ **Victoria Inn & Gardens.** Take time out for afternoon tea, then tour the lush gardens, bayou, and lake, most likely with the inn-keepers' Dalmatians trotting alongside. The rose garden and Shakespeare herb garden are especially fragrant. If you find yourself lingering, why not stay for dinner at the Restaurant at Victoria Inn, featuring superfresh seafood by romantic candlelight? *4707 Jean Lafitte Blvd., Lafitte. ☎ 800/689-4797 or 504/689-4757. www.victoria inn.com. Tea daily 2–3:30pm. Reservations are required; $25 per person (garden tours are free). Restaurant open Wed–Sun 6–9:30pm.*

Where to Stay & Dine

T his is the kind of small town with colorful characters that you'd think only exist in movies or books. It's definitely worth staying a day or two more to mingle with the locals.

Lodging

★★★ Victoria Inn & Gardens.
This is our regular getaway spot from the city ever since we got married here in the Shakespeare Herb Garden. Antique-filled rooms are spacious, well lit, and breezy if you open up the French doors. Innkeepers Roy and Dale Ross and their staff are always gracious. *4707 Jean Lafitte Blvd., Lafitte.* ☎ *800/689-4797 or 504/689-4757. www.victoriainn.com. 14 units. Doubles $110–$145 w/breakfast. AE, MC, V.*

Dining

★★ The Restaurant at Victoria Inn.
Chef Jonathon Lanius only uses locally caught seafood, including shrimp, drum, redfish, crab, and crawfish. Catch your own off the dock and he'll prepare it for you any way you wish. Nothing tastes better! *4707 Jean Lafitte Blvd., Lafitte.* ☎ *800/689-4797 or 504/689-4757. www.victoriainn.com. Entrees $16–$25. AE, MC, V. Wed–Sun 6–9pm.*

★★★ Voleo's.
Yes, everyone is staring at you as you enter this little dive on a dead-end street. Just take a seat at a checkered table, order Paul Prudhomme protégé David Volion's succulent flounder Lafitte, tap your toes to whatever's playing on the jukebox, and you'll stay out of trouble. *5134 Nunez St., Lafitte.* ☎ *504/689-2482. www.voleosrestaurant.com. Entrees $7.50–$14. AE, DISC, MC, V. Mon, Wed–Sat 11am–9pm.*

A typical meal at Voleo's.

Plantations

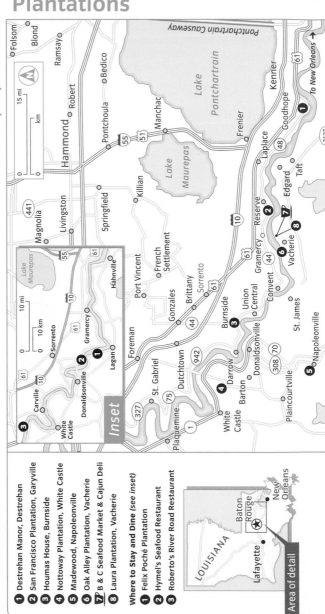

1 Destrehan Manor, Destrehan
2 San Francisco Plantation, Garyville
3 Houmas House, Burnside
4 Nottoway Plantation, White Castle
5 Madewood, Napoleonville
6 Oak Alley Plantation, Vacherie
7 B & C Seafood Market & Cajun Deli
8 Laura Plantation, Vacherie

Where to Stay and Dine (see inset)
1 Felix Poché Plantation
2 Hymel's Seafood Restaurant
3 Roberto's River Road Restaurant

Once plentiful and grand, southern Louisiana's plantation homes are now few and far between. During the golden age of plantation life, from the 1820s to the beginning of the Civil War, plantations were the industrial and social hub for many well-to-do families who relied on slave labor to attain astonishing wealth. In recent years, some plantation tours have begun directly addressing this shameful yet important chapter in our history. **START: From New Orleans, follow Interstate 10 west. Keep in mind that the river winds a bit, so some distances may be deceiving.**

① Destrehan Manor. If you saw *Interview with the Vampire,* you might recognize this elegant mansion built in 1787 by a free person of color as narrator Louis's (Brad Pitt's) childhood home. A meticulous restoration has given it new life but one area was purposely left untouched so that you might better appreciate its survival. ⏱ *45 min. 13034 River Rd., Destrehan.* ☎ *985/764-9315. www.destrehanplantation.org. Admission $15 adults, $5 teens, $5 children 6–12. Daily 9am–4pm.*

② San Francisco Plantation. As you drive past a neighboring oil refinery, it's hard to imagine that this country home was once surrounded by sugar-cane fields. The whimsical architectural style was designed to mimic a steamboat but the bright yellow, blue, and pink hues are true to its Creole heritage.

Inside, look closely at the faux marble and faux wood, popular decorating effects at the time of its construction that demonstrated wealth. ⏱ *45 min. 2646 Hwy. 44, Garyville.* ☎ *888/322-1756 or 985/535-2341. www.sanfrancisco plantation.org. Admission $15 adults, $7 students 13–18, $3 children 6–12. Daily 10am–4pm.*

③ Houmas House Plantation & Garden. Curiously, two homes—one dating back to 1790 and the other to 1840—were joined together under one roof to comprise this enormous estate showcased on 38 acres (15 hectares) of huge live oaks, fragrant magnolias, and perfectly manicured formal gardens. The Bette Davis classic *Hush . . . Hush, Sweet Charlotte* was filmed here. ⏱ *1 hr. 40136 Hwy. 942, Burnside.* ☎ *888/323-8314 or 225/473-7841. www.houmashouse.*

Some visitors may recognize Destrehan Manor from the film Interview with the Vampire, *based on the Anne Rice novel.*

Oak Alley is the quintessential southern plantation home.

com. Admission $20 mansion and gardens, $10 gardens only. Mon–Tues 9am–5pm, Wed–Sun 9am–7pm.

④ ★★★ Nottoway Plantation. Known as the "White Castle," Nottoway survived the Civil War because a Union officer had once stayed there as a guest; you can still see scars from shelling on some of the 22 columns. It's easy to get lost wandering among the mansion's 64 rooms sprawled across 54,000 square feet (5,016 sq. m). My favorite place is the pristine White Ballroom with its original crystal chandeliers and spooky portrait of a grande dame whose eyes seem to follow you no matter where you go. ⏱ 90 min. 30970 Mississippi River Rd., White Castle. ☎ 866/LASOUTH

or 225/545-2730. www.nottoway. com. Admission $15 adults, $6 children 5–12. Daily 9am–4pm.

⑤ ★ Madewood. This place serves as a reminder that revenge is never wise. It was originally built by a man who wanted to outshine his brother, but he died of yellow fever before it was finished. Current owners Keith Marshall and Millie Ball will gladly show you restoration photo albums detailing its transformation from 1960s wrecking ball candidate to glorious Greek Revival masterpiece. ⏱ 1 hr. 4250 Hwy. 308, Napoleonville. ☎ 800/375-7151 or 985/369-7151. www.madewood. com. Admission $12 adults, $5 children. Daily 10am–4pm.

⑥ ★ Oak Alley Plantation. The famous oak-lined drive nearly steals the thunder of the quintessential plantation home. Costumed docents complete the picture-perfect image though their robotic recitations about its history make you wish you were free to explore on your own. ⏱ 1 hr. 3645 Hwy. 18, Vacherie. ☎ 800/44-ALLEY or 225/265-2151. www.oakalleyplantation.com. Admission $10 adults, $5 students, $3 children 6–12. Daily 9am–5:30pm Mar–Oct, 9am–5pm Nov–Feb.

Houmas House.

Laura Plantation out buildings.

7 B & C Seafood Market & Cajun Deli.
This family-owned and operated joint is near Laura and Oak Alley. Order the seafood platter filled with shrimp, oyster, catfish, and crawfish; save room for the bread pudding with sticky sweet rum sauce. *2155 Hwy. 18, Vacherie.* ☎ *225/265-8356. $.*

8 ★★★ Laura: A Creole Plantation.
If you're only going to see one plantation, come here and be blown away by the docents' extensive knowledge and love for this colorful 200-year-old Creole home and grounds. Unlike most plantation tours, they will share the slaves' stories as well and show you the slaves' and overseer's cabins, which were deliberately burned elsewhere so as to "forget" the past. ⏲ *90 min. 2247 Hwy. 18, Vacherie.* ☎ *888/799-7690 or 225/265-7690. www.lauraplantation.com. Admission $15 adults, $5 children 6–17. Daily 10am–5pm.*

Where to Stay & Dine

River Road is famous for its plantations and seafood. Squeezing in as many tours as you can in 1 day can be exhausting. Extend your visit to a night or two so you can enjoy the sights and food at your own pace.

LODGING

kids Felix Poché Plantation.
This 1870 country Victorian home offers a shady porch with river breezes, a French Quarter–style pool, and 22 acres (8.8 hectares) to explore. The private cottages are nice but plain; stay in the main house instead if you prefer richer surroundings. Children are welcome. *6554 Hwy. 44 (River Rd.), Convent.* ☎ *225/562-7728 or 225/715-9510. www.pocheplantation.com. 8 units. Doubles $69–$249. AE, DISC, MC, V.*

★★★ Nottoway Plantation.
Stay the night if you dare; ghosts are rumored to roam the mansion.

Poche Plantation dining room.

The most frequent sighting is that of a young, auburn-haired woman in the girls' wing who resembles original owner John Randolph's youngest daughter, Julia Marceline. If you can afford it, sleep in the master bedroom, which boasts the Randolphs' original furniture, including a hand-carved rosewood poster bed with mosquito netting. Supposedly, valuables were hidden in its hollow posts during the Civil War. *30970 Mississippi River Rd., White Castle.* ☎ *866/LASOUTH or 225/545-2730. www.nottoway.com. 13 units. Doubles $180–$305 w/full plantation breakfast. AE, MC, V.*

kids **Oak Alley Plantation.** View the famous oak trees and National Historic Landmark home from your own private 19th-century cottage. Children are welcome. *3645 Hwy.18, Vacherie.* ☎ *800/44-ALLEY. www. oakalleyplantation.com. 5 units. Doubles $130–$175 w/full country breakfast. AE, MC, V.*

Dining
★★ **kids** **Hymel's Seafood Restaurant.** Owned and operated by the same family for more than 70 years, Hymel's is renowned for its fresh seafood. The warm, casual atmosphere and reasonable prices make it family friendly though it can get noisy at times. Be sure to order the SeaSpud potato, which is topped with real lump crab meat, boiled shrimp, and cheese. *8740 Hwy. 44, Convent.* ☎ *225/562-7031. Entrees $8–$15. MC, V. Tues–Fri 11am–2:30pm, Thurs 5–9pm, Fri 5–10pm, Sat 11am–10pm, Sun 11am–8pm.*

Roberto's River Road Restaurant. The restaurant might not look like much from the outside, but you'll immediately be wowed by the garlic spiciness of the River Road Shrimp inside. (Just don't look too closely at the prices.) *Located on the River Rd. (Hwy. 75) about 3 miles (4.8km) south of Gardere Lane and ¼ mile (.4km) north of Bayou Paul Lane, St. Gabriel.* ☎ *225/642-5999. Entrees $13–$28. MC, V. Open Tues– Fri 11am–2pm, Tues–Thurs 5–9pm, Fri–Sat 5–10pm.* ●

The Nottaway Plantation house.

The
Savvy Traveler

Before You Go

Tourist Offices
New Orleans French Quarter:
Tourist Information Center, 529 St. Ann St., New Orleans, LA 70116. ☎ 504/568-5661 or ☎ 504/566-5031. Near the Hard Rock Cafe ☎ 504/587-0740, on the 400 block of North Peters Street. Vieux Carré Police Station ☎ 504/565-7530, located at 334 Royal St.

New Orleans Uptown: New
Orleans Metropolitan Convention and Visitors Bureau, 2020 St. Charles Ave., New Orleans, LA 70130. ☎ 800/672-6124; www.nomcvb.com.

New Orleans Downtown: New
Orleans Multicultural Tourism Network, 1520 Sugar Bowl Dr., New Orleans, LA 70112. ☎ 800/725-5652; www.soulofneworleans.com. Canal Street and Convention Center Boulevard ☎ 504/587-0739, at the beginning of the 300 block of Canal Street on the downtown side of the street. Close to the World Trade Center ☎ 504/587-0734, at 2 Canal St. Walk-up booths at Julia Street and Convention Center Boulevard and Poydras Street and Convention Center Boulevard.

The Best Times to Go
Traditional seasons don't exist in southern Louisiana. (Local seafood lovers—myself included—insist that the only seasons that count are crawfish, shrimp, crab, and oyster.) In lieu of your plain ol' boring spring, summer, fall, and winter, New Orleans offers two extremes: a hot, humid summer (Apr–Nov) and a relatively mild winter (Dec–Mar).

If possible, avoid visiting the city in July and August, when

Previous page: The St. Charles Streetcar.

temperatures soar into the 90s, thunderstorms pour down every afternoon, and the heat index makes the air feel like you're carrying an extra 20 pounds. Unless you plan on hunkering down in your air-conditioned hotel room or watching countless movies in the cool comfort of a theater, the off-season summer deals aren't worth it. However, winter temps rarely dip below freezing. It's usually in the upper 60s in November, which makes for good walking weather, plus there's green grass and bright flowers year-round.

Hurricane season runs June 1 through November 30 so plan accordingly. August through October is when you see most tropical storm and hurricane action, so if that is a risk you'd rather not take, avoid those few months.

Festivals and Special Events
JAN. Allstate Sugar Bowl Football Classic (☎ 504/828-2440; www.allstatesugarbowl.com) attracts diehard college football fans from all over the country.

FEB. On **Mardi Gras day** (☎ 800/672-6124 or 504/566-5011; www.mardigrasday.com), the entire city is just one big party. The date varies from year to year, but it always falls 46 days before Easter.

MAR. The Tennessee Williams/New Orleans Literary Festival (☎ 504/581-1144; www.tennesseewilliams.net) features readings, theater performances, workshops, and more in honor of Williams, an honorary New Orleanian.

APR. The **French Quarter Festival** (☎ 800/673-5725 or 504/522-5730; www.frenchquarterfestivals.org) is a

Useful Websites

- **Times-Picayune** (local newspaper): www.nola.com
- **The Gambit** (local alt-weekly): www.gambitweekly.com, http://bestofneworleans.com
- **Travel guides for families:** www.bigeasy.com/kids
- **PlanetOut** (Gay & Lesbian travel guide): www.planetout.com
- **Weather reports:** www.accuweather.com, www.weather.com

huge, free music and food fest that warms up crowds for the more famous **Jazz Fest,** the **New Orleans Jazz & Heritage Festival** (☎ 504/522-4786 or 504/558-6100; www.nojazzfest.com). The New Orleans Fair Grounds is transformed into a mass of music stages featuring everything from blues to pop to R & B by little local bands and best-selling artists.

JUL. **Essence Festival** (☎ 800/725-5652 or 504/523-5652; www.essence.com) celebrates African-American culture with music and self-improvement workshops.

SEP. **Southern Decadence** (☎ 800/876-1484 or 504/522-8047; www.southerndecadence.net) brings the gay community together for parades, costume contests, and more.

NOV–DEC. The **Celebration in the Oaks** (☎ 504/483-9415) is a festival of lights set among the giant oaks that can be viewed on foot, by car, or by horse-drawn carriage.

Cellphones

It's a good bet that your cellphone will work in New Orleans, but the U.S. has a very fragmented GSM (Global System for Mobiles) wireless network, so take a look at your wireless company's coverage map before heading out. (To see where GSM phones work in the U.S., check out www.t-mobile.com/coverage.) And be aware that you may or may not be able to send SMS (text messaging) home. You can always rent a phone from InTouch USA (☎ 800/872-7626; www.intouchglobal.com) or a rental-car location, but be aware that you'll pay $1 a minute or more for airtime.

AVERAGE MONTHLY TEMPERATURES FOR METROPOLITAN NEW ORLEANS

	JAN	FEB	MAR	APR	MAY	JUN
High °F	61	64	72	79	84	89
High °C	16	18	22	26	29	32
Low °F	42	44	52	58	66	71
Low °C	6	7	11	14	19	22
	JUL	AUG	SEP	OCT	NOV	DEC
High °F	91	90	87	79	71	64
High °C	33	32	31	26	22	18
Low °F	74	73	70	60	51	46
Low °C	23	23	21	16	11	8

Car Rental

If you plan to hang out in the French Quarter, you're better off walking or taking a cab. It's hard to find parking plus it's expensive. If you truly need a rental car, the best deals are usually found at rental-car company websites, although all the major online travel agencies also offer rental-car reservations services. Priceline and Hotwire work well for rental cars, too; the only "mystery" is which major rental company you get, and for most travelers the difference between Hertz, Avis, and Budget is negligible.

Getting **There**

By Plane

If you fly into New Orleans, you arrive at Louis Armstrong International Airport (Internet airport code MSY), about 25 minutes outside the city. Though smaller than most bus stations, you'll find it an easy walk to baggage claim and grabbing a cab. Need help? Go to the Traveler's Aid Society (☎ 504/464-3522) located in the baggage-claim area.

Getting into Town from the Airport

By Cab

A taxi ride to the French Quarter from the airport will cost you $28 per person for one or two people and an additional $12 each for three or more people.

United Cab (☎ 504/522-9771) is my favorite cab company because they're professional and friendly. I also recommend A Service (☎ 504/834-1400) and Metry Cab (☎ 504/835-4242). Please remember to tip 10% to 15% for good service.

By Shuttle Bus

A cab might be more convenient, but if you prefer a cheaper shuttle bus, go to one of the 24-hour info desks in the airport for a schedule.

For $1.10, the Downtown/Airport Express bus takes you to the corner of Elk's Place and Tulane Avenue— a 30- to 40-minute ride. The bus leaves from the upper level near the down ramp about every 23 minutes from 5:30am to midnight (every 12–15 min. during rush hours). The Jefferson Transit Authority (☎ 504/818-1077; www.jefferson transit.org) can give you more information.

For $15 (one-way), the Airport Shuttle takes you directly to your hotel from right outside the baggage area. For a reservation, call ☎ 504/522-3500. The shuttle is wheelchair accessible.

By Car

If you drive to New Orleans, you'll take one of the major thoroughfares: the Pontchartrain Expressway (Hwy.) 90 or Interstate 10. The former is best if you're heading to the Garden District or Warehouse District; the latter if your destination is Uptown or the French Quarter.

By Train

Your train will arrive at the Union Passenger Terminal (☎ 504/528-1610; www.amtrak.com) on Loyola Avenue in the Central Business District, just a few blocks from the French Quarter. (Interesting side note: the station temporarily served as a post-Katrina jail). Taxis are readily available outside.

Getting **Around**

On Foot
The city is flat, which makes it perfect for walking. Just keep an eye out for large oak tree roots that make for roller coaster sidewalks.

By Public Transportation
Call the Regional Transit Authority's Ride Line at ☎ 504/248-3900 for maps, passes, and other information about streetcars or buses. Any of New Orleans' visitor information centers (including the main location at 529 St. Ann St. by Jackson Square) also have information on public transportation.

The VisiTour pass is a fantastic deal if you frequently use public transportation. It's available at hotels and banks in the Quarter, Central Business District, and along Canal Street in 1-day ($5) or 3-day ($12) increments. Two booths also sell them: one outside the Aquarium of the Americas and the other on the 600 block of Decatur Street. For more information contact the New Orleans Regional Transit Authority (NORTA) (☎ 504/248-3900; www. norta.com).

By Streetcar
Since 1835, the St. Charles Streetcar line has serviced the Central Business District, Garden District, Lower Garden District, Uptown, and Carrollton neighborhoods. The Canal Streetcar line is a 5½-mile (8.9km) ride up Canal through the Central Business District and Mid-City, and ends at one of two destinations, either north on the Carrollton spur to the 1,500-acre (600-hectare) City Park or farther west to the Cypress Grove and Greenwood cemeteries. Both streetcars operate 24 hours a day. Riding either streetcar costs just $1.25 each way (exact change or a VisiTour pass is required). The Riverfront Streetcar line runs along the riverfront from the Convention Center to the French Quarter at Esplanade Avenue. It costs $1.50 (exact change or a VisiTour pass is required). Only the Canal and Riverfront streetcars are wheelchair accessible.

By Bus
Buses connect most New Orleans neighborhoods, though depending on your destination, you'd do best to take the more scenic streetcar when possible. Bus fare is $1.25 (exact change or a VisiTour pass is required). Transfers cost 25¢, and buses are wheelchair accessible.

By Taxi
After dark, I strongly suggest you go with a cab instead of public transportation. Unless it's rush hour, they're easy to find in the French Quarter though you might want to call ahead if you're in a rush. Rates are $4.50 initial charge, plus $1.60 per mile (20¢ per 1/8 mile) thereafter. Add $1 for each additional person. The maximum number of passengers is five. You can also hire taxis for $40 an hour, though taxi companies impose a 2-hour minimum and don't take you outside the New Orleans area.

By Bike
Because the city is flat, you don't need to be Lance Armstrong to bike around. Bicycle Michael's (☎ 504/945-9505; www.bicyclemichaels.com) and French Quarter Bicycles (☎ 504/529-3136) are two good bets for rentals. For maps of bike trails, visit the New Orleans Bicycle Club at www.neworleansbicycle club.org.

By Car

To drive in New Orleans is to be masochistic. Parking is a pain, finding your way is tough because the city's streets follow the twists and turns of the river, and local drivers often make last-minute lane changes and exits. Avoid it if at all possible.

Fast **Facts**

AREA CODE The area code for the greater New Orleans metropolitan area is 504. The North Shore, the region north of the city across Lake Pontchartrain, which includes Slidell, Covington, and Mandeville, is 985.

ATMS/CASH POINTS The **Cirrus** (☎ 800/424-7787; www.mastercard. com) and **PLUS** (☎ 800/843-7587; www.visa.com) networks span the globe; look at the back of your bank card to see which network you're on, then call or check online for automated teller machine (ATM) locations in New Orleans (they're found all over the city so you shouldn't have trouble finding one).

Be sure you know your personal identification number (PIN) before you leave home and be sure to find out your daily withdrawal limit before you depart. Also keep in mind that many banks impose a fee every time a card is used at a different bank's ATM, and that fee can be higher for international transactions (up to $5 or more) than for domestic ones (where they're rarely more than $1.50).

Note: Some small establishments in New Orleans won't take credit cards, so it's always wise to carry a small amount of cash on you.

BABYSITTERS Ask your hotel or call one of the following agencies for sitting services: **Accents on Children's Arrangements,** ☎ 504/524-1227, or **Dependable Kid Care,** ☎ 504/486-4001.

BUSINESS HOURS On the whole, most shops and stores are open from 10am to 6pm. Banks open at 9am and close between 3 and 5pm.

CAMERA REPAIR Try **AAA Camera Repair,** 1631 St. Charles Ave. (☎ 504/561-5822).

CONVENTION CENTER **Ernest M. Morial Convention Center,** 900 Convention Center Blvd., New Orleans, LA 70130, ☎ 504/582-3000. Convention Center Boulevard sits at the end of the Warehouse District, on the river between Thalia and Water streets; the Riverfront Streetcar drops you off at the Convention Center.

DENTISTS Contact the **New Orleans Dental Association** (☎ 504/834-6449; www.nodc.org/noda.htm) to find a recommended dentist near you.

DOCTORS If you need a doctor, call one of the following: **Orleans Parish Medical Society,** ☎ 504/523-2474; **Tulane Medical Clinic,** ☎ 504/588-5800; or **Children's Hospital,** ☎ 504/899-9511.

EMBASSIES & CONSULATES All embassies are located in the nation's capital, Washington, D.C. If your country isn't listed below, call for directory information in Washington, D.C. (☎ 202/555-1212), or log on to www.embassy.org/embassies. The embassy of **Australia** is at 1601 Massachusetts Ave. NW, Washington, DC 20036 (☎ 202/797-3000; www.austemb.org). The embassy of **Canada** is at 501

Pennsylvania Ave. NW, Washington, DC 20001 (☎ 202/682-1740; www. canadianembassy.org). The embassy of **Ireland** is at 2234 Massachusetts Ave. NW, Washington, DC 20008 (☎ 202/462-3939; www. irelandemb.org). The embassy of **New Zealand** is at 37 Observatory Circle NW, Washington, DC 20008 (☎ 202/328-4800; www.nz embassy.com). The embassy of the **United Kingdom** is at 3100 Massachusetts Ave. NW, Washington, DC 20008 (☎ 202/462-1340; www. britainusa.com).

EMERGENCIES For fire, police, and ambulance call ☎ 911. For the **Poison Control Center,** call ☎ 800/ 256-9822. The **Travelers Aid Society** (846 Baronne St.; ☎ 504/525-8726) also renders emergency aid to travelers in need. For help regarding a missing or lost child, call **Child Find** (☎ 800/IAM-LOST (426-5678). If a hurricane threatens, ask your hotel concierge to help you arrange for transportation out of the city. Most hotels no longer allow guests or even their employees to ride out the storm.

GAY & LESBIAN TRAVELERS Gays and lesbians are a vibrant part of New Orleans culture. For information on what's going on in the LGBT community in New Orleans, check out www.gayneworleans.com, and Ambush Magazine (☎ 504/522-8047; www.ambushmag.com).

HOLIDAYS Banks, government offices, and post offices are closed on the following legal national holidays: January 1 (New Year's Day), the third Monday in January (Martin Luther King, Jr., Day), the third Monday in February (Presidents Day), the last Monday in May (Memorial Day), July 4 (Independence Day), the first Monday in September (Labor Day), the second Monday in October (Columbus Day), November 11 (Veterans Day), the fourth Thursday in November (Thanksgiving Day),

and December 25 (Christmas). Also, the Tuesday following the first Monday in November is Election Day and is a federal government holiday in presidential-election years (held every 4 years, and next in 2012). Stores, museums, and restaurants are open most holidays, except for Thanksgiving, Christmas, and New Year's Day.

Note: Mardi Gras day is considered a holiday in the greater New Orleans area and most businesses are closed or have shortened hours.

HOSPITALS Should you become ill during your visit, most major hospitals have staff doctors on call 24 hours a day. However, there are fewer physicians post-Katrina, so after-hours health care may be more limited or require longer waiting periods. If a doctor isn't available in your hotel or guest house, call or go to the emergency room at Ochsner Medical Center, 1516 Jefferson Hwy. (☎ 504/842-3460).

HOT LINES YWCA Rape Crisis is ☎ 504/483-8888; **Travelers Aid Society** is ☎ 504/525-8726; **Gamblers Anonymous** is ☎ 504/431-7867; **Narcotics Anonymous** is ☎ 504/899-6262; **Alcoholics Anonymous** is ☎ 504/779-1178.

INFORMATION The local **Tourist Information Center** is at 529 St. Ann St. (☎ 504/568-5661 or 504/566-5031).

INSURANCE **Trip-Cancellation Insurance:** Trip-cancellation insurance helps you get your money back if you have to back out of a trip, if you have to go home early, or if your travel supplier goes bankrupt. Allowed reasons for cancellation can range from sickness to natural disasters to the State Department declaring your destination unsafe for travel. (Insurers usually won't cover vague fears, though.) In this unstable world, trip-cancellation insurance is a good buy if you're getting tickets well in advance. Insurance policy details vary, so read the fine print—and especially make sure that your airline is on the list of carriers covered in case of bankruptcy. For information, contact one of the following insurers: **Access America** (☎ 866/807-3982; www.accessamerica.com), **Travel Guard International** (☎ 800/826-4919; www.travelguard.com), **Travel Insured International** (☎ 800/243-3174; www.travelinsured.com), or **Travelex Insurance Services** (☎ 888/457-4602; www.travelex-insurance.com).

Medical Insurance: Although it's not required of travelers, health insurance is highly recommended. Unlike many European countries, the United States does not usually offer free or low-cost medical care to its citizens or visitors. Doctors and hospitals are expensive, and in most cases will require advance payment or proof of coverage before they render their services. Though lack of health insurance may prevent you from being admitted to a hospital in nonemergencies, don't worry about being left on a street corner to die: The American way is to fix you now and bill the living daylights out of you later.

For British Travelers: Most big travel agents offer their own insurance and will probably try to sell you their package when you book a holiday. Think before you sign. **The Association of British Insurers** (☎ 020/7600-3333; www.abi.org.uk) gives advice by phone and publishes *Holiday Insurance,* a free guide to policy provisions and prices. You might also shop around for better deals: Try **Columbus Direct** (☎ 020/7375-0011; www.columbusdirect.net).

For Canadian Travelers: Canadians should check with their provincial health plan offices or call **Health Canada** (☎ 613/957-2991; www.hc-sc.gc.ca) to find out the extent of your coverage and what documentation and receipts you must take home in case you are treated in the United States.

Lost-Luggage Insurance: On domestic flights, checked baggage is covered up to $3,000 per ticketed passenger. On international flights (including U.S. portions of international trips), baggage is limited to approximately $9 per pound (1.1kg), up to approximately $635 per checked bag. If you plan to check items more valuable than the standard liability, see if your valuables are covered by your homeowner's policy, or get baggage insurance as part of your comprehensive travel-insurance package. Don't buy insurance at the airport, as it's usually overpriced. Be sure to take any valuables or irreplaceable items with you in your carry-on luggage, since many valuables (including books, money, and electronics) aren't covered by airline policies.

If your luggage is lost, immediately file a lost-luggage claim at the airport, detailing the luggage contents. For most airlines, you must report delayed, damaged, or lost baggage within 4 hours of arrival. The airlines are required to deliver luggage, once found, directly to your house or destination free of charge.

INTERNET ACCESS Three of the most convenient cybercafes are **Cybercafe @ the CAC,** inside the ground floor of the Contemporary Arts Center (900 Camp St.; ☎ 504/523-0990); **Royal Access** (621 Royal St.; ☎ 504/525-0401); and the **Bastille Computer Cafe** (605 Toulouse St.; ☎ 504/581-1150).

LIQUOR LAWS The legal drinking age in New Orleans is 21. You can buy liquor most anywhere 24 hours a day, 7 days a week, 365 days a year. All drinks carried on the street must be in plastic cups; bars often provide one of these plastic "go cups" so that you can transfer your drink as you leave.

LOST & FOUND Be sure to notify all your credit card companies the minute you discover your wallet has been lost or stolen, and file a report at the nearest police precinct (☎ 311). Your insurance company may require a police report before covering any claims. Most credit card companies have an emergency toll-free number to call if your card is lost or stolen; they may be able to wire you a cash advance immediately or deliver an emergency credit card in a day or two. **Visa**'s U.S. emergency number is ☎ 800/847-2911 or 410/581-9994. **American Express** cardholders should call ☎ 800/221-7282. **MasterCard** holders should call ☎ 800/307-7309 or 636/722-7111. For other credit cards, call the toll-free number directory at ☎ 800/555-1212. If you need emergency cash over the weekend, when all banks and American Express offices are closed, you can have money wired to you via **Western Union** (☎ 800/325-6000; www.westernunion.com).

If you lost something at the airport, call **Airport Operations** (☎ 504/464-2671 or -2672). If you lost something at a security checkpoint, call the **Support Operations Center** at ☎ 504/463-2252. If you lost something on the **bus,** call ☎ 504/940-5586, or on the **street-car,** call ☎ 504/827-8399. If you lost something anywhere else, phone the **New Orleans Police Non-Emergency line** (☎ 504/821-2222). You may also want to fill out a police report for insurance purposes.

MAIL The main post office is at 701 Loyola Ave. In the French Quarter, there is one at 1022 Iberville.

NEWSPAPERS & MAGAZINES To find out what's going on around town, pick up a copy of the *Times-Pica-yune* (www.nola.com) or *Gambit* (www.bestofneworleans.com). *Off-Beat* (www.offbeat.com) is a comprehensive monthly guide to the city's evening entertainment, art galleries, and special events; it's available in most hotels.

PARKING In the French Quarter, you're better off in a pricey parking lot rather than risk an illegal spot. If you park on a parade route or block someone's driveway, your car will be towed to the impounding lot (☎ 504/565-7235) or the Claiborne Auto Pound, 400 N. Claiborne Ave. (☎ 504/565-7450). Prepare to pay a hefty fine of $100 or more.

PASSPORTS **For Residents of Australia:** You can pick up an application from your local post office or any branch of Passports Australia, but you must schedule an interview at the passport office to present your application materials. Call the **Australian Passport Information Service** at ☎ 131-232, or visit the government website at www.passports.gov.au.

For Residents of Canada: Passport applications are available at travel agencies throughout Canada or from the central **Passport Office,** Department of Foreign Affairs and International Trade, Ottawa, ON K1A 0G3 (☎ 800/567-6868; www.ppt.gc.ca). *Note:* Canadian children who travel must have their own passport. However, if you hold a valid Canadian passport issued before December 11, 2001, that bears the name of your child, the passport remains valid for you and your child until it expires.

For Residents of Ireland: You can apply for a 10-year passport at the **Passport Office,** Setanta Centre, Molesworth Street, Dublin 2

(☎ 01/671-1633; www.irlgov.ie/
iveagh). Those under age 18 and
over 65 must apply for a 3-year
passport. You can also apply at 1A
South Mall, Cork (☎ 021/272-525),
or at most main post offices.

For Residents of New Zealand:
You can pick up a passport application at any New Zealand Passports
Office or download it from their website. Contact the **Passports Office** at
☎ 0800/225-050 in New Zealand or
04/474-8100, or log on to www.
passports.govt.nz.

**For Residents of the United
Kingdom:** To pick up an application
for a standard 10-year passport
(5-year passport for children under
16), visit your nearest passport
office, major post office, or travel
agency, or contact the **United
Kingdom Passport Service** at
☎ 0870/521-0410, or search its
website at www.ukpa.gov.uk.

International visitors to New
Orleans should always keep a pho-
tocopy of their passport with them.
If your passport is lost or stolen,
having a copy significantly facilitates
the reissuing process at a local con-
sulate or embassy. Keep your passport and other valuables in your
room's safe or in the hotel safe.

PHARMACIES The **Walgreens
Drug Store** at 1801 St. Charles Ave.
(☎ 504/561-8458) is the closest one
to the French Quarter that offers
24-hour pharmacy service.

POLICE For nonemergency situa-
tions, call ☎ 504/821-2222. For
emergencies, dial ☎ 911.

RADIO STATIONS Popular radio sta-
tions include WSMB, 1350 AM
(sports talk); WWNO, 89.9 FM
(National Public Radio, classical);
WWOZ, 90.7 FM (New Orleans and
Louisiana music; jazz, R & B, and
blues); WQUE, 93.3 FM (urban/R &
B); and KKND, 106.7 FM (alt rock).

For local news, tune in to talk radio
station WWL, 870 AM.

RESTROOMS Public restrooms are
located at Jax Brewery, Riverwalk
Marketplace, Canal Place Shopping
Center, Washington Artillery Park,
and major hotels.

SAFETY My rule of thumb is to be
on the offensive. New Orleans'
neighborhoods can change from
block to block so always be aware
of your surroundings. Women
should consider substituting a back-
pack for your usual purse or simply
don't carry one. Public transportation is fine during the day but a cab
is best at night. Avoid the Iberville
Housing Project located between
Basin, N. Claiborne, Iberville, and St.
Louis streets, just outside of the
French Quarter. You should also
avoid St. Louis Cemetery No. 2 near
Claiborne on the lake side of the
Iberville Housing Project unless
you're traveling with a large tour
group. Also stay away from the area
behind Armstrong Park.

TAXES In general, the total sales
tax in New Orleans is 9%; it's 8.75%
in Jefferson Parish.

TELEPHONES For directory assistance ("information"), dial ☎ 411.
Hotel surcharges on long-distance
and local calls are astronomical, so
you're usually better off using a cell
or public pay telephone.

TIME ZONE New Orleans is in the
Central Standard Time (CST) zone.
Daylight saving time is in effect from
the second Sunday in March
through the first Sunday in
November.

TIPPING In hotels, tip bellhops at
least $1 per bag and tip the chamber
staff $1 to $2 per day (more if you've
left a disaster area); the doorman or
concierge only if he or she has provided you with some specific service.
Tip the valet-parking attendant $1

every time you get your car. In restaurants, bars, and nightclubs, service staff expect 15% to 20% of the check, bartenders 10% to 15%, checkroom attendants $1 per garment, and valet-parking attendants $1 per vehicle. Tip cab drivers 15%, skycaps at least $1 per bag, and hairdressers and barbers 15% to 20%.

TRAVELERS WITH DISABILITIES Organizations that offer a vast range of resources and assistance to travelers with disabilities include **Moss-Rehab** (☎ 800/CALL-MOSS; www.mossresourcenet.org); the **American Foundation for the Blind** (AFB) (☎ 800/232-5463; www.afb.org); and **SATH** (Society for Accessible Travel & Hospitality) (☎ 212/447-7284; www.sath.org). AirAmbulanceCard.com is now partnered with SATH and allows you to preselect top-notch hospitals in case of an emergency. **Access-Able Travel Source** (☎ 303/232-2979; www.access-able.com) offers a comprehensive database on travel agents from around the world with experience in accessible travel; destination-specific access information; and links to such resources as service animals, equipment rentals, and access guides.

Many travel agencies offer customized tours and itineraries for travelers with disabilities. Among them are Flying Wheels Travel (☎ 507/451-5005; www.flyingwheelstravel.com) and Accessible Journeys (☎ 800/846-4537 or 610/521-0339; www.disabilitytravel.com).

British travelers should contact Holiday Care (☎ 0845-124-9971 in U.K. only; www.holidaycare.org.uk) to access a wide range of travel information and resources for seniors and travelers with disabilities.

New Orleans: **A Brief History**

1682 French explorer René-Robert Cavelier, Sieur de LaSalle, claims the land near the mouth of the Mississippi and dubs it Louisiana in honor of King Louis XIV.

1718 New Orleans is founded as a valuable port city by Pierre Le Moyne, Sieur d'Iberville, and named in honor of Philippe, Duc d'Orléans.

1762–1800 After Louis XIV gave Louisiana to his Spanish cousin, King Charles III, the French Quarter burned down twice, which explains the Spanish influence on architecture.

1794 Pioneering farmer Etienne de Boré invents a way to extract sugar from cane, which remains a boon crop to this day.

1800 Louisiana is returned to the French.

1803 Napoleon secretly sells the Louisiana territory to the United States, best known today as the "Louisiana Purchase."

1805 The city of New Orleans officially incorporates.

1812 Louisiana becomes the 18th state of the United States of America.

1815 Battle of New Orleans is a pivotal moment in defeating the British.

1832–33 More than 10,000 citizens die during the horrific yellow fever and cholera epidemics.

1837 Mardi Gras is reported on for the first time by the press.

1840 In its glory, New Orleans is the fourth largest city in the country and the second largest port city after New York.

1850 The rampant slave trade makes New Orleans the largest slave market in the nation.

1862 New Orleans is captured by Union soldiers.

1865–77 Time of Reconstruction, when carpetbaggers come in droves and change the city's social and economic dynamic.

1890 Arrested for boarding the "wrong" train, Homer Plessy's decision to sue the state paves the way for landmark segregation legislation, *Plessy v. Ferguson.*

1892 The St. Charles Streetcar goes electric.

1900 Birth of Louis Armstrong, iconic musician, actor, and informal ambassador of all things New Orleans.

1928 Radical populist Huey P. "Kingfish" Long becomes governor of Louisiana, and is then elected to the U.S. Senate 4 years later.

1935 Long is shot at the Louisiana Capitol in Baton Rouge and dies 2 days later at the age of 42.

1938 Playwright Tennessee Williams moves to the Crescent City.

1956 Lake Pontchartrain Causeway, the world's longest bridge, is completed.

1960 Integration of public schools.

1964 The original Canal Streetcar is replaced with buses, which are hit with tomatoes by protesting locals.

1975 Louisiana Superdome opens with great fanfare and mixed reaction.

1977 Ernest N. "Dutch" Morial is elected as the city's first African-American mayor.

1984 Redevelopment inspired by the Louisiana World Expo helps the local economy during the dramatic '80s oil bust.

1988 Famous vampire author Anne Rice returns to her beloved hometown.

2000 The National World War II Museum opens.

2004 After her husband, poet Stan Rice, dies, Anne Rice moves back to California to be closer to her son.

2004 The Canal Streetcar reopens with air-conditioned, handicap-accessible red cars.

2005 Multiple levees break during Hurricane Katrina, destroying a large portion of the city and killing hundreds of people.

2010 Grass-roots organizations, churches, schools, and concerned individuals everywhere continue to help rebuild New Orleans.

Learn the Lingo

Talking the talk and walking the walk are crucial if you plan to go to New Orleans during Mardi Gras. Here's how to sound like a native:

- **Ball** or **Tableau Ball:** Krewes host these themed, masked balls. Themes change from year to year.
- **Boeuf Gras** (fattened calf): The calf represents ritual sacrifice, as well as the last meal eaten before Lent. It's also the symbol of Mardi Gras and the first float of the Rex parade.
- **Carnival:** A celebration beginning January 6 (the 12th night after Christmas) and ending Mardi Gras day.
- **Court:** A krewe's king, queen, and attendants.
- **Doubloon:** Krewes throw these metal coins during parades. They feature the logo of the krewe on one side and its theme for a particular year on the other.
- **Fat Tuesday:** Otherwise known as Mardi Gras, the last day before Ash Wednesday, which is the first day of Lent.
- **Favor:** Krewe members give these souvenirs, which feature the krewe's logo and date, to people who attend their ball.
- **Flambeaux:** Flaming torches carried by parade participants on foot; they aren't members of the krewe.
- **King Cake:** An oval, sugared pastry decorated with purple, green and gold (Mardi Gras colors) that contains a small doll representing the baby Jesus.
- **Krewe:** The traditional word for a Carnival organization.
- **Lagniappe** (pronounced lan-yap): Loosely means "a little extra," and refers to any small gift or token - even a scrap of food or a free drink.
- **Mardi Gras:** French for "Fat Tuesday." Technically, if you say "Mardi Gras day," you're really saying "Fat Tuesday day."
- **Rex:** Latin for "king." The King of Carnival is Rex.
- **Second Line:** A group of people that follows a parade, dancing to the music. Also, a musical term that specifies a particular shuffling tempo popularized in much of New Orleans music.
- **Throws:** Inexpensive trinkets thrown from floats to parade watchers, including doubloons, minifootballs, plastic swords, spears and all sorts of knick-knacks. The most coveted throws are the gilded coconuts of the Zulu Social Aid and Pleasure Club.

Airline, Hotel & Car Rental
Websites

Airlines

AER LINGUS
www.aerlingus.com

AIR CANADA
www.aircanada.ca

AIR NEW ZEALAND
www.airnewzealand.com

AIRTRAN AIRLINES
www.airtran.com

AMERICAN AIRLINES
www.aa.com

BRITISH AIRWAYS
www.british-airways.com

CONTINENTAL AIRLINES
www.continental.com

DELTA AIR LINES
www.delta.com

FRONTIER AIRLINES
www.frontierairlines.com

NORTHWEST AIRLINES
www.nwa.com

QANTAS
www.qantas.com

SOUTHWEST AIRLINES
www.southwest.com

UNITED AIRLINES
www.united.com

US AIRWAYS
www.usairways.com

Major Hotel & Motel Chains

BEST WESTERN INTERNATIONAL
www.bestwestern.com

COMFORT INNS
www.hotelchoice.com

CROWNE PLAZA HOTELS
www.crowneplaza.com

EMBASSY SUITES
www.embassysuites.com

FOUR SEASONS
www.fourseasons.com

HILTON HOTELS
www.hilton.com

HOLIDAY INN
www.ichotelsgroup.com

HYATT HOTELS & RESORTS
www.hyatt.com

INTER-CONTINENTAL HOTELS & RESORTS
www.ichotelsgroup.com

LOEWS HOTELS
www.loewshotels.com

MARRIOTT HOTELS
www.marriott.com

OMNI
www.omnihotels.com

RADISSON HOTELS INTERNATIONAL
www.radisson.com

RITZ-CARLTON
www.ritzcarlton.com

SHERATON HOTELS & RESORTS
www.sheraton.com

WESTIN HOTELS & RESORTS
www.westin.com

Car-Rental Agencies

ALAMO
www.goalamo.com

AVIS
www.avis.com

BUDGET
www.budget.com

DOLLAR
www.dollar.com

ENTERPRISE
www.enterprise.com

HERTZ
www.hertz.com

NATIONAL
www.nationalcar.com

THRIFTY
www.thrifty.com

Index

See also Accommodations and Restaurant indexes, below.

Photo **Credits**

Notes